-268 $2.45
.75 In Canada)

A SPECTRUM BOOK

EDWARD A. WRIGHT

UNDERSTANDING TODAY'S THEATRE

SECOND EDITION

EDWARD A. WRIGHT

is Professor of Theatre Arts at California State University, Long Beach. He has appeared as an actor before audiences throughout the United States and in many foreign countries and has served as a Fulbright Lecturer in Japan. In 1970 he was awarded the Citation of Merit by the *Dictionary of International Biography* for "Distinguished Service as Actor, Author, Director, Teacher of Theatre."

UNDERSTANDING
TODAY'S THEATRE

(Second Edition)

EDWARD A. WRIGHT

A SPECTRUM BOOK

PRENTICE-HALL INC. • ENGLEWOOD CLIFFS, NEW JERSEY

Library of Congress Cataloging in Publication Data

Wright, Edward A
    Understanding today's theatre.

    1.–Theatre. I.–Title.
PN2037.W73–1972   792   72–000008
ISBN 0–13–936245–2
ISBN 0–13–936237–1 (pbk.)

792
W948u

PN2037
.W73
1972

10 9 8 7 6 5 4 3 2 1

Prentice-Hall International, Inc. (*London*)
Prentice-Hall of Australia Pty. Ltd. (*Sydney*)
Prentice-Hall of Canada Ltd. (*Toronto*)
Prentice-Hall of India Private Limited (*New Delhi*)
Prentice-Hall of Japan, Inc. (*Tokyo*)

Contents

THE ACTING & THE ACTORS ✳ 123

THE BACKGROUND & THE TECHNICIANS ✳ 149

RECAPITULATION & RETROSPECT ✳ 168

Preface

My sincere thanks to all those who have permitted themselves to be quoted. Undoubtedly I have borrowed much from other sources without due credit. If this is true, I ask the pardon of the authors and tender them my thanks. In a lifetime of reading all available theatre material, combined with forty years of college and university lecturing and teaching, one tends to merge the opinions of others with his own, and the two become integrally mingled.

I would, however, be remiss if I were not to mention my most inspiring and helpful teacher in drama school—Elias Day—whose brilliant mind and theatre understanding contributed more to my knowledge and love of the theatre than any other single individual. There never was a man who knew, more absolutely, that the theatre is not a pulpit nor a lectern nor a vanity case, but a magical communion between company and audience where, for a little moment, each person gives and receives something beyond himself to create a thing which has never been before and will never be again. So he did not despise the house; he loved it. He did not condescend to theatricality; he delighted in it. He did not scorn emotion; he honored it. He tolerated no disrespect for theatre; but for him it was a joy, not a grim or sacred Cause! Unfortunately, he was too busy during his lifetime to set down any of his thoughts. It is my hope that some of them may be preserved through this work.

Long Beach, California　　　　　　　　　　　　　EDWARD A. WRIGHT

To Louise
who is part of the audience
and without whose
faith, encouragement, and assistance
these pages could not have
been realized.

THE AUDIENCE &
DRAMATIC CRITICISM

INTRODUCTION: A THEATRICAL APPROACH

Understanding Today's Theatre is directed to the audience—that wonderful, unpredictable, and indispensable participant in any dramatic production on stage or screen.

For those who have little or no dramatic background these pages will explain some basic principles that have proved themselves over the centuries and some facts and opinions about the theatre as a synthesis of the arts. A special effort has been made to help the audience distinguish among the substance, form, and technique of the various artists involved in any dramatic production.

A lifetime of active participation on both sides of the footlights, with the commercial and noncommercial theatre, has given birth to many convictions, of which two are dominant. First, audience attitudes can be altered—most theatregoers are anxious and willing to learn more about why they did or did not enjoy a specific experience; and second, the ideal playgoer is a happy combination of intelligence and innocence.

References to specific plays will be kept to a minimum, partly because they are of little value if one is unfamiliar with them, and also because it is our hope that the reader will apply the material to the plays he does know and to the television, motion picture, or stage production he saw last night or last week, arriving at his own estimate of their values—artistic or otherwise.

When, in the mid-50s, the first edition of this book was being written, it was considerably easier to explain how one could understand the theatre, for it was still in the firm grip of what seems to have been the final stages of the "conventional—realistic—well-made play" formula. The goal was always verisimilitude and the complete imitation of surface reality presented with the utmost authenticity in dialogue, action, costumes, and setting. Since the 1860s and Henrik Ibsen, we had taken for granted that all theatre should involve ordinary recognizable people; that all action and the outcome of the plots or stories should be adequately motivated, growing out of the psychology of the characters rather than accidents and coincidences; and that the dialogue should be spoken in plain, colloquial prose. The drama recognized man's many dilemmas, but its basic philosophy was essentially positive.

All who knew and loved the theatre had longed for some alteration. Many sporadic attempts had been made over the years by the avantgarde artists of the day, and some had left their mark on the mainstream, but the basic form still held.

Now the great change seems to have begun. As in all revolutions, a specific date or event can hardly be pin-pointed, but many would trace its roots back to the last decade of the nineteenth century and Alfred Jarry (1873–1907), who is frequently called the grandfather of it all. In 1896 his fantasy of the surrealistic bourgeois character in *Ubi Roi* shocked a placid audience by opening with a four-letter word; it will most likely go down in history as the beginning of open obscenity on the stage. It was Jarry who set the pattern for our modern hippies in his declaration that "every man is capable of showing his contempt for the cruelty and stupidity of the universe by making his own life a poem of incoherence and absurdity." He followed his own precepts and died of drugs at the age of thirty-four in his own world of poverty and filth.

Those who may have found their inspiration in his dramatic concept but who have been more influential and successful in their contributions to this theatre revolution would strive to eliminate all verisimilitude, believing that any realism is incapable of picturing even man's surface reality—much less his basic problems, and that no existing philosophy can explain man's dilemma. In general we have called their work the theatre of the absurd. The dictionary defines "absurd" as "out of harmony with reason or propriety; incongruous, unreasonable, illogical." Ionesco, one of the most prominent playwrights of the theatre of the absurd, says it is "devoid of purpose." Always it is an attempt to project man's metaphysical anguish over the absurdity of the human condition. Logic is ignored, plots or stories are abandoned, individual and realistic characters—even motivations—become unimportant. Its followers adopt the view that life is without meaning, and man must create his own existence from nothing. This meaninglessness is often treated humorously—even to the point of farce—though the absurdist basic view of the world is essentially negative. The theatre of the absurd is sometimes not distinguished from the existentialist theatre, which sees man as free to create himself and to have some impact on the world. Esslin has made the point that, while both share the same metaphysics, the absurd has a greater discontinuity and fragmentation. Sartre as the existentialist and Ionesco and Beckett as absurdists will be discussed further in a later chapter.

Once again we can see that the theatre is immortal, not because it never dies, but because it is always being reborn. When a particular theatre comes to an end because it is no longer useful to its audience, it is replaced by a newer theatre which takes up its work where its predecessor left off.

Yes, our theatre today is in a period of transition so tremendous that it has rarely been paralleled in dramatic history—certainly not in the lifetime of any man alive today. These are interesting times—frequently frustrating—often most difficult to fathom, but for a student of dramatic history there is always that faith that sometime, somewhere, somehow another Sophocles, Shakespeare, Molière, Ibsen, or Strindberg will discover that new formula of success, and once again a theatre with universal appeal will emerge.

Our sincere hope is that we shall live to see that day!

SOME BASIC ASSUMPTIONS AND DEFINITIONS

MAN CREATES THEATRE

Man created the theatre in his own image. He was fully aware that the world was filled with hate, discord, unhappiness, rivalries, misfortune, misunderstandings, conflict, wars, and destruction, but he also knew that there was an abundance of kindness, generosity, love of mankind, brotherhood, fun, excitement, joy, contentment, and personal satisfaction. Symbolically, he chose two masks to represent his creation: a mask of tragedy, that wept, and a mask of comedy, that laughed. For twenty-five hundred years that theatre has persisted. Consistently—almost annually—the world has proclaimed the current season "the worst ever," but this fabulous invalid has defied extinction for all these more than two thousand five hundred years. Its very ingredients have kept it alive, for here man has always spoken to man. They have discussed their joys, their sorrows, their problems, their idiosyncrasies, and their very existence and always in the presence of their fellowmen—the audience. It is that audience to whom we now speak.

3

THE THEATRE'S GOALS

Do you, in your theatre experiences, ask for excitement, emotional release, exaltation, enlightenment, or escape?

The word "entertainment" has been avoided deliberately in the above question, for that is a quality always demanded if we have given of our time and money to witness any form of theatre. Right at the beginning, we want to explain that when someone says, "I go to the theatre to be entertained," he really means, "I go to the theatre for escape," or, "I go to the theatre to be amused."

The word "entertain" comes from the Latin verb *tenere* and means "to hold." Our attention, therefore, may be held by a classroom lecture, a sermon, a prize-fight, a learned debate, an athletic event, or a living-room conversation, for all of these may be highly entertaining. Similarly, we may be as *entertained* by a tragedy, by a modern problem play, or by Shakespeare as by the lightest farce or musical comedy.

In the theatre we *expect* to be entertained! We also expect the artists to communicate whatever it is they wish to say. Through this combination of communication—expression—and entertainment we may enjoy a wide variety of experiences, such as vicarious emotional response; an elation of spirit; the underlining of our own personal convictions or prejudices; a discussion of a social, philosophical, political, or religious concept; the dramatization of stories similar to or vastly different in time and space from our own; or a brief escape from our daily existence through any lighter fare that helps us to forget for the moment the reality about us. All of these goals have been realized in the theatre through its history and still can be today! John Gassner calls them the "Five E's": Express—Entertain—Exalt—Enlighten—Escape.

Have you ever wondered why you were or were not affected by a television, movie, or stage program—or why your friends had a completely different reaction? Can you distinguish between the work of the actor and that of the director? Did you ever stop to ask yourself what the author or costumer, cameraman, scene-designer—even the audience itself—had contributed to the total effect of a dramatic production? Is last night's or last week's—or last year's—play on television, film, or stage still alive in your memory? Would you make an effort to see it again or advise someone else to do so? Why?

This book will try to help answer just such questions, for it is directed to you as one of the Americans who made up last night's audience in the homes and theatres across the country. Whether it was on a television or motion picture screen, an educational, community, or professional stage, you were *part* of that theatre production—in many respects the most vital part. You were an active participant in one of the oldest institutions of mankind—the theatre. You were consciously or unconsciously evaluating the work and the art of all those who had given their best to that performance, working for your enjoyment.

Are you qualified to give an honest or an intelligent judgment of their work? We hope to help you do just that: to assist you in formulating some honest standard of dramatic criticism, to set forth some basic principles that will result in a fairer evaluation of the work of all the artists involved, to make you a better theatregoer.

The theatre is a *popular* (in all its etymological implications) art, and most theatre workers would consider you, the audience, as both their master and their teacher, if not the very reason for the theatre's existence. In 1765 Samuel Johnson wrote:

> The Drama's laws the Drama's patrons give
> For we that live to please must please to live.

You are that giant who stands at the box office or stays away, who turns on or turns off the television switch, and who—alone—determines whether a given program stays on the air. It is you who build the performer's reputation and establishes the popularity of the theatre personality. The great stars of our theatre world stand more in awe of you, the audience, than do you of their prominence, for you are the ones who make that prominence. You will decide when he or she will become a "has-been" as well as when he or she rises to stardom. Without your approval a theatre closes, millions of dollars are lost, artists are discarded.

What have you done, or what can you do, to merit such power and authority? Many will shrug off such a question with the familiar "I know what I like" or "All I want is my money's worth." Greater truth lies in a slight alteration of these phrases so that they become: "I like what I know," and "I get more for my money when I know *why* I have (or have not) gotten my money's worth." In other words, it may not be nearly as important for you, as an individual, to have liked or disliked a work of art as it is for you, a person of intelligence, to know why you did or did not approve, and also to understand why others have or have not done so.

At any rate, it is our purpose in *Understanding Today's Theatre* to go behind the scenes and see something of the art and craft that goes into the writing of the script and the conception and coordination of the director in realizing the total production. We will also point out the personal contributions of the actors and the technicians. We shall present some facts, a number of dramatic principles, and a great many opinions. These should be of help, hopefully, to the beginner in forming some basis for the development of a standard of dramatic criticism that will be fairer to the artists involved and will, at the same time, give the observer a greater enjoyment than is found in looking blindly at what is on view. It is our contention that the greatest enjoyment comes when one realizes why one has or has not been entertained.

We would emphasize that a complete mastery of the following pages will not guarantee dramatic appreciation, for appreciation in itself cannot be taught. It is only a by-product that comes with knowledge and experience. It is our belief, however, that *taste* can be improved, and improving one's taste is a long step toward appreciation. We would define taste as "a mental perception of quality," a perception embodying judgment, a discriminative faculty—the act of liking or preferring something—and the *sense of what is appropriate, harmonious, or beautiful* in nature or art. Both taste and judgment will always be relative, and our goal is not to dictate artistic *fiats*, but rather to make more discriminating the general dramatic taste of the reader. While public feelings can rarely be completely reversed, we do feel that there is within any entertainment medium the power to extend or retard the desires or demands of its audience.

It is not our desire to tell anyone what he should like. *We do not disdain any theatre!* Just as the playwright, director, and actors are striving to please their audience, so we hope to develop an audience for any type of theatre. Such an audience should then be able to evaluate that theatre in terms of its purpose, its meaning, and its success in attaining those goals.

From the start we would admonish everyone that—as does life—education consists of learning the rules; experience teaches the exceptions.

MEDIA THAT MAKE UP TODAY'S THEATRE

We will use the word *theatre* to include television, motion pictures, and the stage.

Today the stage is the theatre of the minority. For many hundreds of years it was the only theatre. The unique thing about the stage is that it is alive and immediate and personal—and these qualities can give it a shattering emotional impact, growing out of the very excitement of playgoing: the proverbial shiver of anticipation when the house lights dim and the curtain is about to rise, the thrill of discovering a fine new play or new talent at a first night.

Though the stage has far smaller audiences than either of the other two media and is today the minority entertainment, it is the parent of them both. In its long history the stage has established many principles and traditions to which the two younger media must adhere. The camera creates by far the greatest single difference between the parent and her offspring. Not only did it make first motion pictures and then television the theatre of the masses, but with it also have come many new techniques. These differences will be pointed out in later chapters.

OUR PREMISE: GOETHE'S THREE QUESTIONS

Since they form the cornerstone of our approach to art appreciation and are the premise to every decision we shall make about the work of any artist in or out of the theatre, we cannot emphasize too strongly the validity and the importance of three questions borrowed from Johann Wolfgang von Goethe (1749–1832):

What is the artist trying to do?
How well has he done it?
Is it worth the doing?

Goethe was the great German Romantic playwright, poet, philosopher, critic, actor, scene designer, costumer, and director of his day. His theory of art criticism has greatly influenced the Western world, though there are those who do not accept it. (Among the dissenters are such prominent and successful critics as George Bernard Shaw, George Jean Nathan, Eric Bentley, and Clive Barnes.) We would request, however, that until the reader has discovered his own theory Goethe's approach be given a fair trial. Regarding the first question, every artist should be conceded the inalienable right to express himself as he desires. We may not agree that his creation is best; we may not like his point of view or his means of expression; we may disapprove of his approach or his personal style; but he is entitled to his creative freedom. To answer the second question fairly we must be familiar with the artist, the period in which he lived, the forms and techniques of the time. The third question demands a sense of values, both taste and discrimination, and a knowledge of theatre.

Although these questions may seem simple—even superficial—one soon realizes that they may be answered on many levels, and the more one learns about any art the more valid they become. Pursued in depth, Goethe's questions give rise to many other questions that require much additional knowledge on the part of the critic. Some of these are listed in a further discussion of Goethe's theory under "Principle Four," on pages 27–28.

IMAGINARY PUISSANCE

Our next assumption is borrowed from the prologue to Shakespeare's *Henry V* and involves an attribute of the theatre known as "imaginary puissance":

> Piece out our imperfections with your thoughts:
> Into a thousand parts divide one man,
> And make *imaginary puissance;*
> Think, when we talk of horses, that you can see them
> Printing their proud hoofs i' the receiving earth.

This concept was further developed by Samuel Taylor Coleridge (1772–1834), who defined Shakespeare's term as a "temporary half-faith which the spectator encourages in himself and supports by a voluntary contribution on his own part." He went on to say that "the true stage illusion . . . in all things consists—not in the mind's judging it to be a forest, but in its remission of the judgment that it is not a forest." Others have called this a suspension of disbelief. This concept is further discussed on pages 33–34 under "Principle Seven."

THEATRICALISM

In a real sense theatricalism is an aesthetic style in its own right just as realism, romanticism, and absurdism are aesthetic styles (see pages 56–61), but it is so integral a part of *all theatre* that theatricalism is usually present in combination with each of the other styles. It is therefore included here as one of the theatre's basic assumptions.

Theatricalism implies exaggeration, something overdone, and as such oftentimes carries a negative connotation. Some would use the word *magnification* to avoid such a reaction. However, we consider it an essential factor in all theatre production and define it as *exaggeration under control*. When used with taste and discrimination it supplies a spirit or quality that enhances every phase of the production. When misused or uncontrolled it is not only a distraction, but can destroy any admirable ideas, emotions, or qualities in the production.

All theatre is exaggeration; it must emphasize and project what it is trying to say. Theatre must be bigger than life if it is to reach an audience. Merely finding the truth is not enough; it must be interpreted and expressed in a distinctive way.

Theatre, according to Aristotle, is an imitation of an action. The very word "imitation" means that what the audience sees can never literally be the real thing; something must have been altered, and it is this alteration that distinguishes theatre from life.

The language used by the playwright, the background that suggests locale, the acting that portrays all emotions and movements—all are composed of artifice, techniques that give only an *illusion* of life. In the currently popular physical contact between actor and audience, participants are conscious of experiencing an *imagined* situation. All are well aware that this audience–actor combination creates a relationship very different from those that exist in reality. The result is still only an imitation of life.

The emotions of life and those experienced in the theatre are essentially the same. However, the methods of eliciting and expressing those emotions and the effects they have on both artist and audience are vastly different. Gassner has defined these two elements as "life's reality" and "theatrical reality." He defines the latter as "making the most of all the theatre's elements" rather than trying to hide or deny them.

Vaudeville, musical comedy, the circus, the opera, and the works of Shakespeare, Molière, and the Greeks never abandoned their theatricality. The clown, Pierrot, Pierrette, Charlie Chaplin's creations, Hamlet, Oedipus, and Tartuffe are supreme examples of theatricalism. Each is theatrical in its own way and in harmony with the dramatic event of which it is a part.

One of the greatest criticisms made of the realistic theatre was of its almost complete abandonment of theatricality. By the same token it has been one of the greatest assets in any avant-garde movement.

One can say things in a play one could not say in any other way— because we know it is "make-believe." Through the arts we can permeate all iron curtains, whether set up by politicians, by ignorance, or by provincialism. It is its very theatricality that makes the theatre so real. The actor can get away with the truth because he does not mean it. Our guard is down. During the German occupation of France, in World War II, the French theatre was allowed to continue. What the underground was able to say through their productions was highly effective in keeping the French spirit alive.

In each of our theatre media today there are many artists—playwrights, actors, designers, and directors—who have, each in his own way, used theatricalism advantageously. Occasionally the motion picture and television screens have given us productions that have been like a breath of fresh air to those of us almost suffocated by this surface realism that denies the theatre's theatricality. To recognize and appreciate the artistry of those who have successfully given us emotional truth through theatrical reality is no small part of the playgoer's responsibility and pleasure.

EMPATHY AND ASETHETIC DISTANCE

In every theatre performance there are two competing forces—each an important part of the spectator's total enjoyment. Adjusting the balance between these two forces is principally the job of the director. (This concept will be more fully developed in chapter 3.) We shall conclude our assumptions and definitions with a brief explanation of these two elements—empathy and aesthetic distance. They are, in varying degrees, a part of any theatre performance, whether conventional or avant-garde, and a full recognition of their effect is essential to our understanding and appreciation.

The dictionary defines "empathy" as "the projection of one's own personality into the personality of another in order to understand him better; intellectual identification of oneself with another." We frequently refer to empathy as "relating to" something. It is a "feeling into"—both muscularly and emotionally.

Aesthetic distance is not the exact opposite by any means, though it does involve a kind of "feeling apart." There is emotional participation, but of a different nature. There is a more intellectual, evaluating atmosphere, which recognizes the work of the artist, while still believing in and being part of what is observed. One is fully conscious that it *is* a play—an illusion. It is evident when we are moved to applaud a splendid piece of acting or a particular line. For example, during a performance of a mystery-melodrama, a dignified middle-aged man became so involved in the situation on stage that when the mysterious hand came through the sliding panel he unconsciously moved forward in his seat and thrust his arm out. In doing so, he touched the shoulder of the young lady who was directly in front of him; she, equally involved, screamed uncontrollably. The dramatic impact was destroyed and the empathy of the audience broken as they were suddenly pulled back from the illusion of reality.

The motion pictures early sensed the values of empathy and aesthetic distance. Every means of playing upon them has been used. Film melodramas have shown as much surface realism and as much of the physical reactions of actors as possible through the use of the close-up. Dramatic scenes are brought so close to an illusion of reality that little is left to the imagination. A glance to right or left during a particularly strong sequence will show the contorted faces of the audience, the clenched hands or other overt physical responses. If one has been too involved in the situation to make this observation, one need only recall the muscular tension felt when a scene dissolved or faded into one that suddenly changed the emotion. The motion pictures have also found great use for aesthetic distance and detachment in the musical extravaganzas, huge spectacles, and historical panoramas where they excel so brilliantly.

In contrast there is the broken rapport born of distractions or monotony. It may be caused by a flickering lamp, a forgotten line or missed cue, a false cry or laugh, an extraneous sound, unstable furniture, or a characterization that is false. Sometimes this broken rapport is caused by the audience itself—through coughing, an audible comment, the arrival of latecomers, or some exterior element such as that illustrated in the mystery-melodrama cited above.

In this area, television has a serious handicap with its regular breaks for commercials, and having to play against a background of domestic distractions.

One of the sharpest contrasts between the avant-garde and conventional theatres is in their use of these two elements. Brecht, in striving for alienation on the part of the audience, *increased* the aesthetic distance at the expense of empathy. He made his audience conscious of all the theatrical effects and at the same time tried to involve them *intellectually* with the stage action, thus creating a desire to act to eliminate the social wrongs being depicted. In another wing of the avant-garde there are those who would completely *destroy* aesthetic distance by moving the actors into the audience and *physically* involving the spectators in the production—even to the point of assaulting them. This is a vastly different use of empathy from that desired in the illusion of the realistic theatre.

It is important to understand the dramatic power inherent in both empathy and aesthetic distance and in the manner in which they are employed in each production.

THE SPHERE OF THE CRITIC

No other art and its participants are so freely criticized by the inexperienced and the inept as the theatre and those who create it. Each man, woman, and child considers himself a just critic of what he has witnessed in a theatre. Though he may refuse to discuss the worth of a musical composition, a painting, the lines of a cathedral, or any of the other arts, none will hesitate to evaluate a dramatic production. He will speak glibly of the play and the acting and oftentimes the setting. This is perhaps the price the theatre must pay for speaking the language of the common man and for being the most democratic of the arts. The would-be critic's opinions may be the result of prejudice, meager knowledge, lack of understanding or sensitivity, momentary admiration or dislike for some individual participant, a poor dinner or disposition, an auditorium too hot or too cold, or of countless other extraneous influences, but he attaches the emotional reaction to the production itself. In addition to being ill-founded, these criticisms are often off-the-cuff. Who has not heard, accepted, repeated, and been affected by such generalizations as: "They say it is terrible!" or "They say it is terrific!"

We have no serious objections to such comments when they are the outgrowth of honest study and observation and are accompanied by specific reasons. It is therefore the material that will enable people to make a more honest evaluation that we try to present here.

George Jean Nathan once said: "Dramatic criticism is an attempt to formulate rules of conduct for that lovable, wayward, charming, wilful vagabond that is the drama." It is just such rules or principles that we shall try to discover. Let us hope that with them the reader can avoid becoming the critic who feels he must always find a little that is bad in the best of things.

John Gassner wrote: "Dramatic criticism consists of describing the interaction that occurred during a dramatic performance when each of the three entities—the script, the production, and the audience—acted and was acted on by the other two." Our goal will be to explain what the playwright and those involved in the production were attempting to accomplish.

The following lists of requirements and obligations are directed primarily to the individual who may find it necessary to *write* a review or criticism and thus report on his total reaction. Some of the items will be repeated under "Principle Seven" on pages 31–34 where we define the good playgoer, but there our main concern is with the individual who attends primarily for his personal enjoyment.

REQUIREMENTS OF THE DRAMATIC CRITIC

(What he brings with him to the theatre)

An abiding love and respect for theatre.

As broad a background as possible in the history of theatre and dramatic literature. A knowledge of many plays.

A wide experience with life on many levels.

An acquaintance with people and their relationships.

Taste and discrimination.

An understanding of the form and techniques of the artists.

The ability to recognize creative talent and to distinguish between genius and mediocrity.

A sincere appreciation of what the theatre has been and can be.

A thorough knowledge of his own prejudices.

OBLIGATIONS OF THE DRAMATIC CRITIC

(How he uses his knowledge and experience)

To view each dramatic event with an ample supply of imaginary puissance.

To recognize and discount his own prejudices.

To observe and evaluate the work in all areas of the production.

To give each artist the right to express himself as he desires.

To ask always the three questions of Goethe:

What is the artist trying to do?
How well has he done it?
Is it worth the doing?

To report on the audience reaction, especially if it differs from one's own.

To give reasons to substantiate all conclusions about individuals and about the total production.

To be objective, honest, forthright, and fair before attempting to be clever.

LEVELS OF DRAMATIC CRITICISM

In a very real sense dramatic criticism can be said to exist on at least three levels, which we shall define as the literary, the theatrical, and the practical.

The literary approach, sometimes called the Aristotelian, emphasizes primarily the literary value inherent in the written drama. Critics have used this approach in a variety of ways—always with greater emphasis on the script than on the production. Some are most interested in the play's philosophical or sociological aspects; they are principally concerned with its impact upon and contributions to the individual's life and his relationship to the world, his problems, and associations with his fellow men. Others are more interested in the aspects of the script that involve form, style, structure, language, characterization, and originality, or in the technique with which all of these have been put together.

A third critic may approach a play from the viewpoint of history, taking into account the period in which the drama was written and first performed, the size and shape of the physical theatre, and the evolution of the playing area and seating arrangement, as well as the varying demands and moods of the audience during the centuries of the theatre's existence.

In each instance, this first level of dramatic criticism is primarily concerned with the written drama, the work of the playwright, and is less interested in its theatrical effectiveness and popularity with the audience.

The second level asks what the theatre can do for the drama when it becomes a play, how well it can be enacted, what its psychological impact can be in production. Its practitioners evaluate the script as a theatre-piece as well as a literary work. They are primarily interested in the theatre magic that can be experienced through actors, scenery, lighting, sound, and audience.

The third level is concerned primarily with a play's commercial value —how much money it will make—how popular it will be, and how long it will run. This is sometimes called "the Shubertian" approach, a name derived from the famous New York producers who for many years made a business of the theatre. It is the criticism most frequently leveled at the commercial theatre, motion pictures, and television.

To be fair, one should recognize and evaluate individually the various levels: the greatness in drama, the creation of aesthetic enjoyment through theatrical magic, and popular entertainment. All three can be found in a single production. Unfortunately, sometimes none are present. More often than not there are variations of value even on the same level, and frequently a vulgar piece pretends to be better than it really is. Tinsel, spectacle, and applause can easily mislead us.

In summary (this statement will be developed and explained in later pages): the work of each artist should be measured by the originality, truth, imagination, and sincerity of his conception and by the unity, emphasis, rhythm, balance, proportion, harmony, and grace of its realization.

PITFALLS IN ANALYZING DRAMATIC PRODUCTIONS

One danger in dramatic criticism lies in the tendency among some critics to cite picayune details and minor accidents in performance instead of searching for the real dramatic values. If ever the old expression about not seeing the forest for the trees is applicable, it is here. The untrained critic is apt to pounce on such small mishaps as a fluffed line, a delayed light cue, a prop not wholly authentic, some slight discrepancy in make-up, a frayed seam on a costume, or some similar detail not worthy of mention. If such instances have been so numerous or so blatant as to denote carelessness on the part of the participants or to distract from the plot, theme, acting, setting, or direction, that is another story. In such a case, criticism is justified. First nights in any theatre are often chaotic affairs. The nervousness of the entire company and their awareness of the importance of the event often produce many unforeseen accidents, but discerning critics never allow them to sway their opinion of the production as a whole.

This tendency to seek out the small flaws is typical of the novice, but there are seasoned playgoers and professional critics who never really seem to enjoy a dramatic event—they are so involved in looking for something wrong that they miss all that is valuable and positive in the art itself. These unfortunate souls become so wrapped up in their own reactions that they fail to see the play.

The intelligent playgoer soon finds that this is only an early phase in his development. Soon he ceases to be preoccupied with details and begins to study the production as a whole. Then criticism takes its logical place and becomes a factor in greater theatre enjoyment. Similarly, he becomes aware that the word *criticism* need not mean censure, for the honest critic may also praise.

The cardinal rule for the beginning dramatic critic should be to have some good reason for whatever opinion he may express. Generalizations —whether approving or disapproving—are far more valuable if founded on specifics.

In a written criticism he should never tell the story, although he may explain the theme or aim of the play. He should take for granted that the reader has not seen the performance and reveal nothing that might mar his enjoyment of the play. Finally, the critic is wise to avoid the use of technical or dramatic terms that are not apt to be known by the average reader.

A critic should always be as objective as possible in his reporting. Where emotion is involved, objectivity is very difficult, but he should at least report the reaction of the audience—especially if it has differed from his own. It is not his duty to say what should have been done, for he is not necessarily a creative artist. He is a reporter presenting his own opinions on the artistic merits of the occasion. He need not mention everyone concerned but should single out individual efforts that were outstanding in one way or another. It is his duty to be straightforward—to make up his mind—to speak his feelings, whatever they may be, honestly, forthrightly, sincerely. "The best dramatic criticism," Burns Mantle once said, "is like writing a letter home."

While a dramatic evaluation may carry more weight because it appears in the morning paper and may seem more authentic because of the prestige of the writer, it is not necessarily more honest or of greater value than that of the average theatregoer—if that individual possesses some basic theatre knowledge and has conscientiously followed some honest set of principles of dramatic criticism. In each instance it is only one man's opinion.

In concluding our discussion of the critic's responsibilities and obligations, we offer our "Ten Commandments of Dramatic Criticism." Some of the areas may not be wholly clear at this point, for they involve discussions presented in the following chapters. The first five are concerned with the critic himself. The second five are concerned with the work of the various artists involved in the production. Attention to these ten statements should produce an intelligent and honest evaluation of a dramatic production.

TEN COMMANDMENTS OF DRAMATIC CRITICISM

1. I must constantly—in all my theatre experience—use "imaginary puissance."
2. I must know, understand, evaluate, and discount my own prejudices.
3. I must evaluate each of the five areas and the work of all artists involved in the production.
4. I must measure the entire production in terms of life and understand what each artist has personally contributed of himself to make or mar the production.
5. I must arrive at every decision only after using Goethe's three principles of artistic criticism.
6. Each artist must make crystal clear what he is trying to say by means of proper emphasis, sincerity, and projection.
7. Each artist must work within the medium at hand or successfully adapt any elements borrowed from another medium.
8. Each artist must cooperate with the others and coordinate his work toward a single goal, which is the purpose of the production.
9. Each artist must be wholly believable as he interprets life through his own personality.
10. Finally—the production may move me, stir me, excite me, amuse me, teach me, or transform me, but the one thing it *dare not do* is bore me. The one thing it *must do* is send me on my way somehow better equipped to face or to understand life.

All the verbs used in commandment 10 have been carefully chosen, for it is a basic tenet of our particular theory of dramatic criticism that the theatre exists on many planes and can be many things to many people. There is ample room in the world of theatre for *The Odd Couple* and *Waiting for Godot,* for *Auntie Mame* and *Long Day's*

16

Journey Into Night, for *Charley's Aunt* and *Mother Courage,* for *Three Men on a Horse* and *Hamlet,* for *Blithe Spirit* and *Oedipus Rex,* and for all the levels that lie between—be they conventional or the most extreme of the avant-garde.

SOURCES OF INFORMATION

In our efforts to understand the theatre better we shall rely on three sources of information: *facts, opinions,* and *principles.* The remaining chapters of this book will fall into one or another of these three categories. We must recognize each source for what it is and understand its value to the theatre in general and to us personally. To this end it is most helpful to read the works of theatre artists and craftsmen who have written about their beliefs and their experience.

To know that a certain person made a certain statement is to know a fact; the content of that statement, however, may be only his opinion. When an individual accepts for himself another's opinion, it becomes a principle for him. One's dramatic principles are always changing with time and experience—just as the principles of the theatre are changing. However, at any given time, our evaluations of a production grow out of the principles we have established for ourselves.

FACTS

Facts are the most easily recognized. The simplest examples are dates, definitions, pictures of actual productions, the names of playwrights, actors, and technicians, the stories of plays, and the provable effects that certain individuals or works have had on dramatic literature or theatre production. Familiarity with as many plays from as many countries and periods as possible is desirable.

The following statements may be considered to be facts:

Our Western theatre has its origin in the culture of the Greeks; it was part of their religious life some five hundred years before Christ. Aeschylus, Sophocles, Euripides, and Aristophanes were four of the greatest Greek playwrights.

The Elizabethan Age in England, during the latter part of the sixteenth century and early part of the seventeenth, was one of the greatest literary eras of the English-speaking people, and William Shakespeare was its leader.

Henrik Ibsen, a Norwegian, considered to be the father of the modern drama, wrote his greatest plays between 1860 and 1905. He was the author of such socially significant plays as *The Doll's House* and *Ghosts,* which were effective in bringing about changes both in contemporary attitudes toward life and in the laws of our land.

The motion pictures are less than one hundred years of age and television is less than fifty, but the stage has been an important part of and influence upon our Western civilization for over twenty-five hundred years.

More people in this country can now say on any given morning: "I saw a play last night" than at any time in history, for at least 95 percent of our American homes have television sets, millions of people were present in motion-picture houses, and thousands were seeing stage productions by school, community, or professional groups across the country.

OPINIONS

Of the three sources of information, *opinions* are the most debatable, as well as the most interesting and challenging. In the *opinions* of excellent scholars, the turning point of *Hamlet* has been variously placed in three different scenes: (1) the players' scene, when Hamlet is finally convinced that the king is guilty; (2) the scene where he could revenge his father's death by killing the king but does not; and (3) the mother's bedchamber scene, either when the ghost makes his second appearance or when Polonius is killed. The proponent of each opinion based his defense of it upon his own principles.

If opinions vary so widely on a written script, it is little wonder that agreement by the best critics on a total production is rare indeed. Opinion on the most ephemeral of the theatre arts—acting—is usually so varied that a single characterization by a given actor may evoke the full gamut from "deplorable" to "brilliant," and the same vocal quality or physical action may be described as "sheer genius" or "amateurish and regrettable."

Listed below are a number of opinions chosen from prominent drama theorists. They represent champions of the conventional theatre as well as the avant-garde—though some belong to the avant-garde of other times. As opinions the following may evoke some interesting discussions:

"Who ever said the theatre was created to analyze character, to resolve the conflicts of love and duty, to wrestle with the problems of a topical and psychological nature that monopolize our contemporary stage?"

—*Antonin Artaud, 1938*

"People never truly laugh except when they are together—he who weeps at a play is alone; and the more deeply he feels, the more genuine is his pleasure, especially in the Serious Drama, which moves us by true and natural means."

—*Beaumarchais, 1767*

If [the drama] be an ordinary mirror, a smooth and polished surface, it will give only a dull image of objects, with no relief—faithful, but colorless,—every one knows that color and light are lost in a simple reflection. The drama therefore must be a concentrating mirror, which instead of weakening, concentrates and condenses the colored rays, which makes of a mere gleam a light, and of a light flame. Then only is the drama acknowledged by art."

—*Victor Hugo, 1827*

"There should no longer be any school, no more formulas, no standards of any sort; there is only life itself, an immense field where each may study and create as he likes."

—*Émile Zola, 1873*

"A play should lead up to and away from a central crisis, and the crisis should consist in a discovery by the leading character which has an indelible effect on his thought and emotion and completely alters his course of action."

—*Maxwell Anderson, 1938*

"The aim of avant-garde plays is to re-discover and make known a forgotten truth—and to re-integrate it, in an untopical way, into what is topical—it is obvious that when these works appear they cannot help being misunderstood by the majority of people."

—*Eugène Ionesco, 1964*

"Tragic feeling is evoked in us when we are in the presence of a character who is ready to lay down his life, if need be, to secure one thing —his sense of personal dignity."

—*Arthur Miller, 1949*

"Once you assert that the meaning of life is absurdity, that the laws of logic are spurious, that action is meaningless, that individuality is illusory, that social interaction is unimportant, and that communication is impossible, you have denied every assumption upon which the art of the theatre as we have known it in the Western world is based."

—*Robert W. Corrigan, 1964*

"It seems that the closer we move to actual life, the further we move away from the drama.—Drama purely imitative of life isn't drama at all."

—*Sean O'Casey, 1956*

"In art we are concerned, not with mere imitation, but with the imposition of some form upon the material which it would not have if it were merely copied as a camera copies."

—*Joseph Wood Krutch, 1929*

PRINCIPLES

Each of the opinions listed above has become a *principle* for the theorist quoted. It is valid for him, but not necessarily for others.

We may sometimes find ourselves in disagreement about a given artist's work or about the worth of a total production. Before any discussion becomes too heated we should seek the lowest common denominator, which is the principle upon which each is basing his conclusions. The fact that certain principles are suggested on these pages does not mean that the reader must accept them, but they can be used as a first step toward building his own standard of criticism. We would, therefore, ask that the seven basic principles that follow serve—for the present—as a foundation upon which we shall hope to build a structure of theatre understanding. These principles, we feel, are a valid start for any beginner who is interested in learning more about the theatre. They try to answer the following questions:

1. What is Art?
2. Of what is Art composed?
3. What is the purpose of Art?
4. How can I understand or evaluate Art?
5. Why is Theatre an Art?
6. What are the Theatre's obligations?
7. What are the obligations of the audience or the critic?

> *Principle One: Art Is Life Interpreted By and Through the Personality of the Artist.*

George Jean Nathan once said that if he were the Secretary of Culture he would burn all the books that attempted to define art. If such a ruling were to be enacted it would greatly reduce our libraries; indeed, we could fill many pages by listing what has been written in an effort to define art. For our purpose, the definition listed above seems most satisfactory. In the theatre every artist endeavors to picture life as he sees it. We credit two men for the definition. Francis Bacon said: "Art is man added to Nature"; the great Japanese playwright and storyteller Chikamatsu Mongaemon (often called the Japanese Shakespeare) said: "Art is the layer that lies between the skins of truth and falsity— that which is false but not false, true but not true—that is what gives us joy."

Man's experience is not limited to the things he can see, hear, or touch. Unlike other animals he has the power to picture in his mind what is not but what might be. He is able not only to accumulate, record, and profit by the experiences of the past, but to imagine and devise different ways of doing things—to have new ideas.

All art implies selection on the part of the artist. The moment that man enters any situation we have the twin elements of *selection* and *emphasis* rather than sheer representation, for man interprets, and no two persons see exactly the same picture. When man begins to create, to record, or to communicate what he has seen or felt *as he has experienced it*, art begins. He adds something to nature, and the result is neither true nor false, although the illusion may seem more real than life itself.

No artist is ever wholly natural—he only *seems* natural. The most interesting conversation in life could very well be unreal or unsatisfactory in the theatre, lacking emphasis, coherence, unity, climax, or continuity. The very characters we might shun in life are frequently found to be the most delightful or entertaining on the stage.

Let us imagine for a moment that an individual has had an experience in life that has given him great personal pleasure by affecting him either emotionally or intellectually. It may have been the discovery of a great truth, the realization of a philosophy, the appreciation of the beauty of a sunset, the song of a bird, or some humorous or serious aspect of daily life. In any event, the participant has an all-consuming desire to reproduce that experience so that it can be shared with others. He must first choose the art through which he will speak. What he wants to share may be most easily expressed by the dance, by a musical composition, a poem, a formal painting, or a cartoon. He could choose the short story, the novel, or the drama. Let us imagine that he has chosen and written the drama. Readers of this drama may find in it what the playwright meant to say, or they may discover some further experience of their own that they, too, wish to share. They produce the drama, which then becomes a play, and they in turn become actors, technicians, and director. In the work of each artist some facet of his own thinking, feeling, and background will appear, for the tree an artist paints is not nature's tree—it is his. The characters a playwright creates are not life's characters—they are his. St. Joan, Queen Elizabeth I, Abraham Lincoln, and Mary of Scotland have appeared countless times in literature. Each re-creation is different, although patterned after the same model, for each is the sum total of a different author's impression, technique, and imagination. In the art of acting, twenty Hamlets will be twenty different people, although they speak the same lines, for each actor must create the character through his own experiences and personality.

Every artist selects and emphasizes just what he desires us, his audience, to see, and we, therefore, see life through his eyes. The playwright tells his story within his chosen framework, with characters, dialogue, and theme all slanted to portray life as he sees it. The actor creates the role in terms of his own physical, emotional, vocal, and intellectual qualifications. The various technicians do what must be done to sustain the mood, project the story, and enhance the quality of the production. Simultaneously the director as creator, interpreter, and coordinator translates all these elements into a harmonious whole. All work toward the same goal—to share an emotional experience by picturing some aspect of life through their own personalities and to give the audience a memorable experience.

In the arts, we who make up the audience are given the opportunity of submitting to new and varied experiences, of momentarily stepping out of the world of reality and knowing the worlds that are inhabited by the great artists of the ages. We see life, for the moment, through their eyes and their personalities.

{ *Principle Two: Art Consists of Three Specific Elements—Substance, Form, and Technique.* }

An artist's substance is what he tries to communicate—his conception or dream, his content or subject matter, the aspects of life he wishes to emphasize or express, the emotions, feelings, moods, or ideas he would share with his audience. The artistic value of this substance is measured by its *originality*, its *truth*, its *imaginative quality*, and its *sincerity*—four attributes that should be constantly in mind as one studies any work of art.

To project these feelings or thoughts the artist must give them shape or form. Only through some form is he able to project his substance. That form may be a poem, a short story, a novel, a painting, a sculpture, a dance, a drama, or any other art expression.

If the artist has chosen the theatre—whether as playwright, actor, director, or technician—he will be concerned with such items as type, style, spirit, purpose. He must select the form that will best express or communicate the emotion or mood he hopes to project. The correct form will intensify what he has to say and thus enhance his content.

Though each individual art work has its own demands, each artist must consider what are called the *pillars of the fine arts—unity, emphasis, rhythm, balance, proportion, harmony,* and *grace*. While these pillars must be recognized in studying the work of each individual artist, they are given special consideration in this book under The Direction & the Directory (chapter 3, pages 119–21), for in our theatre it is the director who in his production must strengthen whatever may have been neglected by playwright, actor, or technician.

Form is sometimes said to involve certain rules, formulas, standards, conventions, or patterns. Whatever term we may choose, history has proved many times that the conventions of a form do change and that rules or principles must not confine an art—even though every art does constantly produce rules. At a given time they constitute the structure within and by which an artist creates. When he can be more effective by altering them or even by establishing a new form, he should do so.

It has often been said that we should neither violate basic principles for the sake of novelty nor have so great a fear of breaking these principles as to paralyze the creation of beauty. This concept has resulted in the dichotomy of thinking with which we view our divided theatre today. The avant-garde playwrights are striving to find new means of expressing themselves. The opposition feels that their substance and especially their form are either wholly lacking or not given sufficient importance. The avant-garde champions would contend that the substance is there but is not as photographically or realistically presented—that the real substance lies beneath the surface—is more metaphysical and dependent on a greater intellect or imagination. They would also point out that there is a form—a *new kind of form*. They could quote Victor Hugo, an avant-garde playwright of another day who in 1827 was crying out for a new theatre to replace the neoclassicism of the time and who said: "There are two sorts of models, those which are made according to the rules, and, prior to them, those according to which the rules are made."

It was not until almost one hundred years after Aeschylus, Sophocles, and Euripides had completed their works that Aristotle analyzed the playwrights' masterpieces and wrote his *Poetics*, which for centuries stood as the guide for other playwrights. In time, Shakespeare and his fellow dramatists created an entirely new style of playwriting by disregarding the unities and formal rules of the Greek dramas. Thus a new form was established, and the Romantic style was born. Again, in the mid-nineteenth century the realistic drama became the most popular style and has persisted for a hundred years through many new styles—Strindberg and his expressionism, Zola and his naturalism, Maeterlinck and his symbolism, and some less successful efforts before World War I as surrealism, Dadaism, and other styles. Such innovations were the avant-garde of their day, and each had its effect, though none very much altered the main stream of the realistic theatre. Only since World War II has it been seriously threatened, as we shall show in the next chapter. The theatre is a most pragmatic art. What works is good, and what works is eventually accepted and thus becomes the theatre of the period. The only requirement is that the results be equally—or more—effective than they would have been with the form that the artist has altered or forsaken. The dramatist today is only using another arrangement of the same ingredients that were used by Sophocles, Molière, Shakespeare, and Ibsen, and this new arrangement reflects the spirit of the times.

The playwright with his words and meter speaks through the elements of drama: theme, plot, dialogue, mood, character, and spectacle. The play he writes will usually, although not always, fall into one of the four general types of drama—tragedy, melodrama, comedy, and farce—or perhaps some combination of these. His style may be classic, realistic, romantic, naturalistic, impressionistic, fanciful, epic, surrealistic, absurd, and so on. The structure of his script may include some or all of the following: exposition, inciting moment, turning point, falling action, climax, and conclusion. When the script is brought to life in the theatre before an audience each contributing artist expresses himself through a form that is a part of his contribution to the total production.

The actor's approach represents the school and method he has chosen for his involvement with the technical, intellectual, and emotional areas of acting. The scene designer's form is reflected in the style of his scenery. It may be realism, simplified realism, impressionism, expressionism, or a combination of several. The costumer and the electrician have worked within certain bounds or conventions demanded by their fields. Even the director will have approached the whole production with an overall design that encompasses certain principles or traditions. There is no final authority, no absolute standard, in the theatre, but there are principles that must be given recognition if the finished product is to show the planning, foresight, care, and selection that great art possesses. We recognize that there are some recent philosophies that do not agree, but it is our opinion that real art is never unpremeditated, that art cannot exist without meaning, objectivity, and organization. Thomas Mann defined literature as the union of suffering with the instinct of form. All art is carefully worked out and designed by the artist, and this premeditation is the form through which he expresses his ideas or emotions.

Technique is the third element and it involves the fitting or blending of the substance into the form. It is the artist's personal means of accomplishing his end and calls for the selection and arrangement of the artist's materials for a particular effect. Form and technique are the elements that differentiate art from life. Technique distinguishes one artist's work from that of another; it is sometimes called his personal style or quality, for it is essentially the artist's projection of himself. The three media—stage, motion pictures, and television—are very much alike so far as substance and form are concerned, but they vary greatly in their techniques.

Two actors could not possibly play a role identically, nor could two playwrights write the same story in the same way, although both of them may deal with the same subject and follow the same principles—principles dictated by the form which has been selected.

Alexandre Dumas *fils*, the French playwright, once said: "Technique is so important that it sometimes happens that technique is mistaken for art." We are all familiar with stage, motion-picture, and television personalities who depend too much on their technique or showmanship for success. Such artists usually have a very short professional life, for substance and form are, in the final analysis, more important. Technique without content is not enough—an artist must say something. In the chapters dealing with the playwright, the director, the actors, and the technicians, we shall further distinguish among these three components of an art, for it is fundamental that one must have a knowledge of the various forms and techniques common to drama and theatre production, both past and present, if one is to understand the artistry of any dramatic production.

{ *Principle Three: The Purpose of All Art Is To Communicate the Artists' Thoughts or Emotions; To Give Aesthetic Pleasure and To Clarify or Help Us Understand Life.* }

Count Leo Tolstoy said:

Art is a human activity which is passed on to others, causing them to feel and experience what the artist has felt and experienced. . . . It is a means of communication between people, uniting them in the same feelings. . . . As soon as the spectators and the hearers are affected by the same feelings which the artist felt—that is art.

Communication may be mental, emotional, or spiritual. Attempts to relate the experience fully or to transfer the ecstasy are oftentimes futile. This most valuable aspect often cannot be explained because the deeper meaning of any work of art is subjective. Whether the artist speaks to many or to few depends upon the art and is a debatable issue. A critic once wrote that if the artist was able to transfer to only one other person the essence of what he felt or experienced, he had created a work of art. This theory is known as the Mandarin view: as art becomes greater, it is understood and appreciated by fewer and fewer people. Proponents of the Mandarin view use the phrase, "the higher the fewer," while their opponents contend that if the audience is so limited, the artist's communication is not as clear as it should have been; that art is universal. They would point again to Tolstoy who said: "Exclusive art is bad art. Good art unites."

The physical experience of beauty, which lifts us out of ourselves and enables us to see more deeply into the great realities, has been called aesthetic pleasure. It is the stimulation of the imagination through the senses and the result is an appreciation of the beautiful.

Beauty has never been absolutely defined. Some feel that the artist merely records the beauty that is inherent in his subject matter. Others believe that beauty lies in the artist's personal style or technique in duplicating nature. Some would call it a "unity in variety" or the complete harmony of all the elements that the artist has used to express a central idea or theme.

Many moderns contend that beauty exists in the mind of the viewer or hearer, that the artist strikes some note that brings to the observer's mind a pleasurable experience or emotion, giving aesthetic pleasure through recognition of a past experience. Another theory places the sense of beauty in the artist's personal interpretation of what he sees.

There are also some who unite their ethical or religious thinking with their aesthetic sense. Closely allied, but standing by themselves, are those who can derive aesthetic pleasure only when they perceive the presence of God or an emphasis on their own moral code combined with their art. In the theatre these individuals are often called the moralists, for they insist upon the presence of a great moral theme or lesson.

Certain intellectuals say that aesthetic pleasure can come only from an art object that challenges them to think or furnishes a greater understanding of the world's problems. We contend that there is as much beauty in our theatre today as at any time in all history. We would not for a moment be classed with those pessimists who feel that the theatre is dying or those who constantly cry for the "good old days" and protest that "the theatre is not what it used to be." We agree with the man who said that poetry exists at that moment when one becomes conscious of the presence of the beautiful. By such a definition poetry certainly did not go out of the theatre with the death of Shakespeare or Jonson. It has only changed its emphasis. In many respects there is more poetry in some of our modern theatre than in Shakespeare's day. His poetry lay in the written text of the script; ours can lie in the complete harmony of all the arts that are found in a dramatic production.

Aristotle wrote: "The aim of art is to represent not the outward appearance of things, but their inward significance—this, and not the external mannerism and detail, is true reality."

Life and art each have much to tell us, but the artist chooses some single truth and through his selection and emphasis is better equipped as a teacher to make it clear.

We may not like the way in which he has portrayed his feelings or thoughts; we may question the values involved. Indeed, we may even debate whether or not they should have been expressed. We should, however, be clear as to the artist's purpose, his feelings, and his thoughts. We should feel that we know what he has been trying to say. This does not mean that someone else may not get from the work another idea or a different emotional response. People's backgrounds, points of view, and mental processes are so different that we frequently interpret the same work differently from other people. A *play should be a movement toward something*. To permit an audience to leave the theatre without a clear idea of what that something is, or not knowing what the play is about—even if it is about doubt or nothingness—is not good art.

There are two kinds of obscurity. One is unfathomable; the other provides a depth that furnishes a greater understanding as one returns to the work time and time again with new thought and maturity. *Hamlet* is a play that does this. The story can be simply told, but it has challenged the minds of scholars and philosophers for more than three hundred years. The theatre—more than any other art because it is directed to more than the individual—should possess a clarity that is less necessary in a poem, a painting, or even a novel, all of which are addressed to the individual.

If it is not always possible to clarify life's problems—and some of our recent playwrights feel this is unnecessary if not impossible—the theatre should, at least, help its audience better to understand life and to recognize that their burdens might be equalled or surpassed by others. Hopefully, this realization can offer at least a rationalization, if not some small satisfaction.

> *Principle Four: A Valid Premise to Any Artistic Evaluation Could Logically Consist of the Three Questions of Goethe: "What Is the Artist Trying To Do? How Well Has He Done It? Is It Worth the Doing?"*

What is the artist trying to do? What type of script has the playwright provided? Is it tragedy, melodrama, comedy, farce—or a combination of any of these? Is his goal sheer escape for the "tired businessman," or would he teach us some lesson? Is the play purely a commercial venture, or does it represent an effort at an artistic and worthwhile document? Has he chosen to amuse, instruct, propagandize, convince, delight, enthrall, excite, startle, or otherwise arouse his audience? In what style has he written? Has he used the conventional structure of the "well-made play"? What elements of drama have received his greatest attention? Does he have a theme? What questions does he raise or answer? To what age or cultural level does he appeal?

Has the director used the original text, an adaptation, a revision, a translation? Was the choice a wise one? Has he altered the playwright's emphasis on plot, character, mood, or theme? Has he cast wisely? Has the text of a familiar play received the director's own interpretation, an entirely new one, or the conventional one? Does the director seem to have emphasized the theme projected by the author? How has he treated it—seriously, facetiously, with tongue-in-cheek, lightly, satirically? What aesthetic or personal style is seen in the production? How has the director balanced empathy and aesthetic distance, reality and theatricality? How has he treated the production in terms of color, line, mass, pace, rhythm? How has he used sound, lighting, and scenic effects to tell his story?

Has each technician cooperated with the director's interpretation yet brought to the production his own particular gifts and talents? Have any of them detracted from or especially added to the production? Is any element in the designs symbolic?

Have the actors been impersonators or interpreters? Have they exploited their own personalities? Are they well rehearsed, adequate in imagination, vocal and physical training, emotional impact? What has each individually brought to the performance? Are they playing subtly, broadly, in a specific style? Are the characters drawn or played as stereotypes? Do the actors work as part of an ensemble? Are they fresh, easy, restrained, convincing? Do they mean to be?

How well has he done it? This is the critic's opportunity to judge the degree of success the artists have achieved. Here we appraise their methods, their talent, and their success in attaining goals such as those we have recognized in the first question. We are now concerned with the effectiveness of the whole production, and that effectiveness is measured by the principles that we have chosen as yardsticks for ourselves. They are the measure of the dramatic knowledge we now use in evaluating the artist's personal form and technique as outlined in "Principle Two."

Is it worth the doing? Again the goal of the artist is brought into focus, but now we raise the question of value in time and effort on the part of both artist and viewer. We may ask: Was the script or production worth the time of the author—of all those involved? Did it merit the audience's time and money? Has the same thing been said or done too many times before or done better? Is the piece stageworthy? Has it added to the stature or experience of any of the participants? Has the performance helped anyone in any way? Has it been done too often or too recently in this area? Was it worth reviving? Does it promote theatre in general or raise theatre standards? Was its very purpose worthwhile?

> *Principle Five: The Theatre Is a Meeting Ground of All the Arts and as Such Consists of Five Areas—Drama or Script, Actors, Technicians, Director, and Audience—Each of Which Must Be Given Full Consideration.*

For many years the fine arts were considered to include dance, music, poetry or literature, sculpture, painting, drawing, and architecture. Some of the more recent publications of standard dictionaries have listed an eighth—dramatic art. Whether or not this becomes common practice is unimportant, for even a casual analysis of the elements that compose the seven fine arts will point up the fundamental truth that the theatre is perhaps the one place where all the elements of all the arts meet on common ground—the *bodily movement* and *gesture* of the dance, the *rhythm, melody,* and *harmony* of music, the *meter* and *words* of literature, and the *line, mass,* and *color* of the space arts—sculpture, painting and drawing, and architecture. Surely, then, the theatre is a synthesis of the arts. With today's emphasis on the total dramatic production and the unification of all its elements, the theatre, whether a separate art or a synthesis of the arts, is subject to the tests of unity, emphasis, rhythm, balance, proportion, harmony, and grace, which we recognize as the pillars of the fine arts.

This is a book about understanding *theatre* rather than *drama*. The drama, or written script, is only one part of a theatre production. There are many nonliterary elements involved in the play. The crafts, as well as the arts, become important ingredients as the actors, technicians, director, and audience are brought into the total picture. Furthermore, a play is made for many people. The written script is only a drama and does not become a play until it is performed on a stage by actors and before an audience. The theatre is a genuinely cooperative art.

The theatre today may be compared to a five-ring circus. Until all five rings have been seen and judged, we have not really seen the production. These five aspects include the playwright, the actors, the technicians, the director, and the audience. In many respects the audience is the most important of all the contributors, for author, actors, technicians, and director have from the beginning been working for the satisfaction, the approval, and the entertainment of that audience.

These areas, and all they embrace, are the elements of the theatre. Until the theatregoer has recognized and honestly judged the contributions of every artist involved, he has not really seen the play.

> *Principle Six: The Theatre, as a Synthesis of the Arts, Exists for the Audience and Has Specific Obligations to That Audience Whose Time and Money It Accepts.*

The theatre must always make its appeal to the whole audience rather than to the individual. It belongs to the people and should exist for and speak to them.

This responsibility need never discourage experimentation, growth, or change. On the contrary, it may stimulate them, for audiences are willing to learn and are ever seeking something new. Although audiences have always been receptive to change, the theatre artist, more than any other, may be compelled to move slowly. He must never forget that he is the servant of the many.

The true lover of the theatre would criticize both the producers and directors who cater to the lower dramatic taste and follow the slogan "give the audience what it wants," and those who would sacrifice entertainment to their own pet theories of "art for art's sake" or "social significance." One asks too little of the audience and the other too much. Either will soon know only a disappointed and diminishing audience, for the theatre should be an institution in and of itself rather than an extension of the platform, the pulpit, or the classroom.

The theatre is first a cathedral of emotion. If it can teach a truth of life, inspire the audience to do finer things, thrill them with poetry or literary quality, or challenge them intellectually, then the experience has been truly worthwhile. Horace said wisely in 34 B.C.: "He who joins the instructive with the agreeable, carries off every vote by delighting and at the same time admonishing." The theatre must give its audience an emotional experience. One *feels* greatness before recognizing it intellectually.

It is the further obligation of the theatre to give the audience far more of life than its members could have lived in the period of time they spent in the theatre. It must accent the lessons and truths it presents, paint the characters or situations so vividly that the audience may come to know or live them. The story may parallel or may differ radically from life as experienced by the audience, but it must always furnish the vicarious experience and emotion that only the theatre can give.

Man has until recently demanded that the theatre as an art *seem* real rather than *be* real, that it *reflect* life and not *be* life. It is in this element of seeming that we find the art of the theatre, although the exact degree has varied throughout the ages and among the many types and forms of theatre. Shakespeare's admonition: "Hold the mirror up to nature," supposes a special kind of mirror—one that reflects for the audience just what the artist would have it see and feel. John Gassner has called this "theatrical reality."

A fourth obligation of the theatre is always to make the audience *believe* what it sees—at least for the time being. The light of the morrow and the process of careful analysis may reveal certain implausibilities, but these must never be obvious during the performance. The emotion, spirit, and illusion of life must be present.

Finally, the theatre must at all times seem to tell the truth about its people and about life. As Voltaire said: "The stage is a lie; make it as truthful as possible." Ironically, we can, through a lie, present a truth of life! This does not mean that plays and settings must be realistic in their style, or even that the subject matter must be close to actuality. A fantasy can be just as true as the most realistic play if the characters in that fantasy and the setting against which it is played are *consistent with the laws of their imagined existence. The Tempest* and *The Blue Bird* are just as true as the most literal representation of life, and their truth may be far more lasting in our memories.

To summarize, the theatre's five obligations to its audience are:

To appeal to the audience rather than to the individual.

To move its audience emotionally.

To give its audience more of life than they could live in the same period of time.

To *seem* real as it creates an illusion of life.

To create an illusion that must be a truthful picture of life and that the audience must believe—at least while in the theatre.

> *Principle Seven: The Audience, as Part of the Total Dramatic Experience, Has Certain Obligations to the Artists Who Make Up the Theatre.*

Throughout these pages the audience is foremost in our thoughts. Every artist works in the hope of sharing an experience with the audience, of bringing to it some measure of entertainment to which the audience will in turn give its sustained attention and immediate appreciation. This sought-for attention and appreciation make the audience an active participant in any dramatic production; it is as much a part of the success or failure of a production as is the contribution of any theatre artist.

The theatre has been described as a strange combination of imagination and reason. The nature of the ideal audience is half childlike, half adult, knowing something of both literary and stage values, but above all, possessing a respect for the theatre as an institution and as an art. Only then will an audience, like a child, give tangible evidence of its pleasure, its sympathy, its delight, and its exaltation. This giving is imperative if the fire of ecstasy is to be kindled for both actors and spectators.

The variety of what this audience may most appreciate is unlimited. Some may desire the lines of Sophocles or Shakespeare, and others the lines of today's most popular motion-picture actress. One may choose a play that propagandizes some religious or social theme, and another an historical romance or biography. To some a ballet of pretty chorus girls backed by spectacular scenery and accompanied by lively music may have a far greater appeal than a play by Ionesco or the latest edition of *Hair*. One may clamor for revivals of the classics or a dramatization of a famous novel, while his neighbor would prefer the naturalness of Chekhov or the obscurity of Genet. There are always those in attendance who would find their greatest pleasure in the preachments of Shaw, Artaud's "Theatre of Cruelty," the epic theatre of Brecht, the searchings of Pirandello, or the theatrical intellectual challenge demanded by Eric Bentley. Practically every theatre audience will include some of all these individuals.

Someone has divided the theatre audience into three extremes—the escapists, the moralists, and the artsakists. First, there are the escapists who want only to forget the responsibilities and problems of their everyday lives. They ask only to be amused and they cry out for the lighter plays and musicals. They are referred to as the "tired businessmen," although they are found in all professions and sometimes, surprisingly enough, among our most brilliant minds.

Not long after *Death of a Salesman* had completed its road tour, a professor from a large university was heard to condemn the play because it had haunted him for days and he seemed not to be able to put it out of his mind. When asked why he had not liked the play, his answer was: "It had nothing to say." Those within hearing were quick to point out that it said a great deal, that its theme showed that a man who builds his life and that of his family on a foundation that is both shallow and ethically unsound is doomed to failure. The professor readily agreed that he had found all that in the play but that what troubled him was that there were too many people exactly like that in America. This was an even more astonishing revelation, for it meant that he had completely shut his eyes and mind to the fact that people might sense the theme and realize their own errors before it was too late. Then came the answer that should have been foreseen had it not come from so distinguished an educator: "To tell you the truth, when I go to the theatre, I want something light and entertaining."

The second audience group includes those who demand that the theatre must always uplift, teach a lesson, preach a sermon, picture some part of life of which they personally approve. They close their eyes to anything with which they do not agree. Either they blind themselves to the fact that evil does exist in the world, or they refuse to accept the theatre as a reflection of life. In either instance, they are being honest neither with themselves nor with the artists whom they would criticize. This group we may call the *moralists*.

The third extreme includes those theatregoers who insist on "art for art's sake." They shudder at box-office success and disdainfully refer to all popular theatre as "show business." They deny that the theatre belongs to the people and claim it for their own little esoteric group. They imply that popularity with an audience is an indication of mediocrity and far beneath the true artists. These individuals we call the *artsakists*.

The *good* playgoer does not look upon the theatre as merely a temporary vacation from his own personal problems. He asks that it be more than mere escape, and he puts no limitations on the artist's conceptions or beliefs but permits him to use whatever material he may need to tell his story. He does not demand any particular style of entertainment—other than that it be good theatre, whether it is the work of a clown, a *Hamlet*, a tragedy of Sophocles, or slapstick comedy. When he enters the theatre, he makes a certain surrender to it—but not a blind surrender, for he retains his judgment and his taste. He accepts the theatre as make-believe, as a world built for him by many people, all participating in an effort to picture something of life by way of the artist's conception, and he, as part of the audience, will try to evaluate these efforts.

The *good* playgoer realizes that the theatre is a synthesis of all the arts and that many individuals are responsible for the production he is to witness. He does not think only in terms of the story, or the actors; or the scenery, or the lighting, or the costumes. He realizes that he may like some part of the production and be disappointed in another; and that it is unjust to condemn or praise the whole because of some single contribution. He appreciates the fact that the theatre is capable of moving him in many ways; that it can stir, excite, amuse, teach, or transform, but that the whole experience is a two-way proposition—a game that he, too, must play.

He knows that at the very heart of all theatre pleasure is what Shakespeare called "imaginary puissance"—a sort of temporary half-belief. (See page 8, "Some Basic Assumptions.") This half-belief does not demand that he blindly say, "That is Hamlet's castle" or "That is the home of Willy Loman"; it asks only he does not insist that it is *not* Elsinore or the home of Willy Loman.

The *poor* theatregoer is sometimes disturbed when he sees people he knows playing parts that are contrary to his accepted beliefs, as in the case of the college professor who said to the director: "Please don't ever cast one of our fine young people in an objectionable role, for always afterward one is reminded of that character when he meets him on the street." He refused to give each actor the right as an artist to be an actor and to speak the lines of someone else.

Contrary to this narrow and wholly unjustified viewpoint, the good playgoer gives the actors, the scenic artist, and all those involved with the production the opportunity of taking him into their imaginary world. When these actors, these technicians, and this director have failed to accomplish their goal after the playgoer has given them ample opportunity through his imaginary puissance, then he has the right to offer whatever adverse criticism of them as artists he may desire. It will show more intelligence on his part, however, and give him greater personal pleasure if he is able to tell *why* they have or have not failed to accomplish their goals.

The good playgoer recognizes his own personal prejudices and tries to rise above them. He may not care for a given actor or for a particular type of dramatic event, but he does make an effort to judge each honestly by giving every artist his right to work as he chooses.

The reader will do well to understand the five basic obligations summarized below, for they are the *minimum* essentials for being a good theatregoer. They are a repetition of the first five items listed under "Obligations of the Critic" on page 8. (As we pointed out there, the critic, whose work may appear in print, has additional responsibilities.)

OBLIGATIONS OF THE THEATREGOER

To view each dramatic event with an ample supply of imaginary puissance.

To recognize and discount his own prejudices.

To observe and evaluate the work of all areas of the production.

To give each artist the right to express himself as he desires.

To ask *always* the three questions of Goethe:

> What is the artist trying to do?
> How well has he done it?
> Is it worth the doing?

Finally, we emphasize that a unanimity of opinion regarding any performance is neither possible nor desirable. Agreement or objectivity where emotion is concerned is not expected. Even with the same set of principles two persons will arrive at widely different opinions about the work of any artist. This is a result of many factors, a few of which are: different backgrounds and emotional temperaments, personal interests, level of maturity, and the basic fact that none of us can see nor hear with the eyes or ears of another.

It is our conviction that we, the audience, cannot adequately answer Goethe's three questions until we have recognized the distinction between the substance, form, and technique of each theatre artist. We must have some familiarity with the form and principles that have been established over many hundreds of years before we can understand either the old or the new. We must learn to appreciate the artist's personal style and technique, which have helped him to blend the substance into the form of his art. Only then can we appreciate the originality, talent, and imagination that have brought forth something that is peculiarly his own.

Such appreciation is intellectual growth at its best, for education is something that happens inside the individual and depends as much upon what that person brings to it and what he is as it does upon the facilities provided. It involves:

Mastery of some basic principles and the vocabulary of a given area.

Knowledge of where to find further relevant information.

The use of these by a mind sufficiently disciplined to analyze and think for itself.

The very spirit of education is to assist the individual in realizing his own potentialities, to help him discover what he really can do—not as imitation, not in response to command, not because it has been charted for him, but because he has acquired a new view of himself and his capacity.

After all, the only authentic education is what remains in the form of appreciation, refined tastes, attitudes, and disciplines long after the specific facts have been so thoroughly absorbed that they may be beyond the range of ready recall.

One distinction that can be made between the educated man and the cultured one is that the former is able to collect, file, and recall a great many facts, while the cultured man uses them by applying them to the world around him.

HOW WELL HAS HE ACCOMPLISHED IT?——

THE PLAYWRIGHT'S SUBSTANCE

The story he is trying to tell
The theme he is trying to proclaim
What he is trying to say to us, to make us feel or understand
His treatment of material: literary, theatrical, or journalistic; moral or immoral

□ *His tools:* plot, theme, mood, characters, dialogue, spectacle

THE PLAYWRIGHT'S FORM

The type of play he has chosen
The aesthetic style he has used to suggest or imitate life

THE PLAYWRIGHT'S TECHNIQUE

The structure of his play
His blending of theme and plot
His personal style
His strategy and tactics
Tests of greatness

—— WAS IT WORTH THE DOING? ——

THE PLAY AND
THE PLAYWRIGHT

In the work of three "conventional" dramatists—Ibsen, Chekhov and Shaw—and four "avant-garde" playwrights of their day—Strindberg, Pirandello, Brecht and Ionesco—one may find the complete range of what the modern theatre offers.

DEFINITION AND SUBSTANCE

The written manuscript of the play is referred to as "the script." A drama does not actually become a play until it is brought to life by actors before an audience. The very spelling of the word—*playwright*, rather than *playwrite*—should indicate that a play rather than being written, is *made* by the contributing efforts of those who are responsible for the full production. The written drama is a most complex organism with an identity all its own.

The playwright must, in his presentation, constantly think in terms of how the words will sound to the ear rather than how they will look on the printed page. He must omit descriptions, write in terms of action or movement, and be constantly aware of the pictorial effect as well as the rhythm of speech. He must know the physical limitations of his theatre and realize that clarity is vital, for the audience is not able to ask questions or to go back and reread a speech to make sure of what was being said. The characters he creates and the philosophies, ideas, actions, and problems he pictures must be vital and interesting. In short, everything must be theatricalized, but the degree of this theatricalization will depend on the particular form and technique chosen by the playwright.

Historically, the dramatist has created for the physical arrangement of his contemporary theatre, and this has largely determined both his substance and his form. Consequently, we have known the majestic beauty of the Greeks, who wrote for huge outdoor religious spectacles, the poetic power of the Elizabethans, the brilliant repartee of the Restoration, the artificiality of the Victorians, the man-in-the-street or next-door-neighbor ordinary conversation of the twentieth-century realistic theatre. A greater appreciation of any script is realized when we are aware of the time and theatre for which it was written.

Many years ago someone facetiously defined a play as a trap which the characters were either falling into or struggling to get out of—a statement with much truth, for drama is a situation in motion, demanding action, discovery, and change. Early in this century Clayton Hamilton more satisfactorily described a play as "a story devised to be presented by actors on a stage before an audience." This seemed to be an adequate definition until a small group of playwrights began to eliminate the element of "story" and some productions abandoned the stage as such and used the audience area for the performance as well. Their innovations were so successful with many audiences that these new concepts ceased to be mere experiments and became part of an *accepted* theatre, if not the conventional one. It would seem wise, therefore, to enlarge Mr. Hamilton's definition by saying that "a play portrays some aspect of man's existence dramatized to be presented by actors in a theatre before an audience."

It has been said that drama is the most perfect instrument man has devised to record, vitally and in dimensions, the mystery and magic, the purpose and pattern of his life through the ages. It has also been called the "conscience of man" speaking to its fellow men.

In our opening chapter we said that a play was a movement toward something. That something is the *substance* of a script. It can be an idea, a philosophy, an emotion, a story, a character, or a truth. It can create a mood, mirror nature, present an old idea in a new way, propagandize, picture the human spirit, depict the nature of the times, or whatever else the dramatist may choose.

In our discussion of the substance, form, and technique of the playwright, we shall—as much as possible—include both the conventional and the avant-garde. However, since the specific goal of the latter is to alter or break with that which is established, this group will be given special consideration. (See page 69). (See page 69)

Nevertheless, in the broad sense of what the theatre tries to accomplish, much of what is said is equally valid for the work of every playwright. For century after century, just as today, he has endeavored to answer through his substance some aspect of the four eternal questions:

What is the nature of man?

What is man's purpose in living?

What is man's destiny?

What is the good life?

Since the beginning of Western drama in ancient Greece, the playwright has had certain tools with which to work. In Aristotle's *Poetics* (322 A.D.) they were *fable, manners, sentiment, diction, melody,* and *scenery.* In modern times they have been called the six elements of drama and include *story, character,* and *thought,* which are expressed through *dialogue, mood,* and *spectacle.* In different periods and by specific playwrights these elements have been given varying degrees of importance. Some chose to emphasize story, others the characters, and some the theme. There are excellent scripts in which mood or dialogue hold the greater prominence. Generally speaking, the sixth—spectacle— has been considered to be of less literary value and used only when some of the other five have seemed not to be sufficiently present. Spectacle might consist of mob scenes, beautiful costumes, dance extravaganzas, battles, elaborate stage pictures, or some other superficial addition. Today, in some of the more avant-garde scripts, spectacle has taken over and become the most dominant of these items in the form of rock or electronic music, slides, film strips, sound tapes, exotic lighting, fireworks, obscenity, nudity, and other means of stirring or shocking the audience.

Aristotle further emphasized that tragedy was an imitation of an action; the characters should reveal themselves by what they did; the action should be worthy and illustrious, with a certain magnitude and expressed in pleasing language; tragedy should effect purgation through pity and fear; it should possess a beginning, a middle, and an end, with a unity of action and a reversal of fortune wherein the leading character should pass from ignorance to knowledge through some recognition in himself or others; and while the historian might write of particulars and things as they were, it was the province of the poet to write of things as they might be.

During the Renaissance of the sixteenth century Aristotle was rediscovered and, though frequently mistranslated, has had the greatest influence of any single person on the theatre throughout the ages. Only in very recent times have the non-Aristotelian forces received more than casual attention.

Along with the principles of Aristotle the Renaissance discovered reason as the means of understanding man and the forces that surround him. Cause and effect became the manifestations of a coherent universe. It was established as a basic premise that man was a creature capable of dignity, who could live best in a world of human rationality, and that his life was worth living. All these concepts were woven into the texture of the theatre and became a part of what has come to be known as the conventional theatre.

Between 1850 and 1900 four theorists altered the world and brought about the greatest innovation in the substance of the drama that has yet been known. They were Charles Darwin, with his revolutionary findings in the physical and religious worlds; Karl Marx, in the social and economic; Sigmund Freud, in the sexual and psychological; and Friedrich Nietzsche, with his philosophical origination of the "God is dead" theory. They struck at the very foundation of the theatre's basic concepts.

With these findings the concept of the dignity of man was destroyed as was the concept of his personal mastery of his own destiny. Guilt and the superiority of the Ego were all but eliminated. It is largely as a result of these discoveries that we have, in modern literature, very few great tragedies and none that can stand beside *Hamlet, Oedipus Rex, Electra, Macbeth, King Lear*, and other masterpieces.

New questions were asked, such as:

Why is there evil in the world?

Why do the innocent suffer?

Why should man's best efforts and superior intelligence meet with disaster?

Why should we submit to laws that are indifferent, blindly mechanical, or malicious?

Partly in an effort to answer these and similar questions there appeared during the late nineteenth century "the drama of ideas," which continues to the present. Playwrights have followed, among others, three different approaches to their goals—the thesis play, the problem play, and the propaganda play. They are difficult to separate, for the lines of demarcation are very thin and one is often merged into another. In general, however, the *thesis play* presents a problem—social, politicial, or moral—that the playwright would have us consider. He argues a solution to the issue. Ibsen and Shaw excelled in the thesis play. They were convinced that society needed improvements, which were necessary to man's happier existence.

The *problem play* simply states the problem and offers no solution. The playwright shows a certain detachment as he studies the whole question pro and con.

The *propaganda play* cites a problem and presents and argues for the particular solution the playwright desires; but it goes one step further in trying to stir the observer into immediate action. This kind of play later became known as *Agit-Prop* (Agitation-Propaganda).

THREE APPROACHES: LITERARY—THEATRICAL—JOURNALISTIC

These approaches and the plays that use them have brought forth a new approach to evaluating the playwright's substance. Is it journalistic, theatrical, or literary?

A journalistic play is one written for a given audience, time, or theatre, because the subject seems to be popular. The vast majority of scripts seen on television in any season deal with one of several subjects: specific professions, crimes, detective stories, westerns, mystery plays, historical pieces, foreign intrigues, and aspects of science fiction. There is a demand, so the playwright rushes to his typewriter and tries to satisfy that demand. Externally motivated, these "plays" serve the same purpose as journalism. The audience is waiting for a particular program much as they await the daily newspaper. The playwright writes because the public wants him to speak, and his work is as dated tomorrow as yesterday's headlines. The motion pictures and the stage are also susceptible to this appeal.

The purely theatrical play, on the other hand, may last for several years, will bear seeing a number of times, and will be revived by another generation. It may not read as well as one would hope, but it does play well in the theatre. It has suspense, characterization, excitement, good dialogue, and some truth or theme to give it stability and meaning. Such a play is frequently referred to as "good theatre."

The literary piece always has some inkling of eternity. It belongs not to a particular day or period, although its plot may stem from an incident or a specific date. The literary play achieves originality without attempting to be novel or unusual. Its goal is not so much to shock its audience (although, as with Ibsen, it frequently does) as to reveal some truth that the author must share with his audience. Journalism seeks to be timely, the theatrical to be exciting. Both approaches are more interested in facts—often box-office facts. The literary man is interested in facts not as facts but as they represent recurrent truths of human existence. The literary playwright writes from an inward impulse. He has something to say and he must say it. Tennessee Williams summarized it very well: "To snatch the eternal from the desperately fleeting is the great magical trick of human existence."

Playwrights have different goals. Occasionally a drama may possess two or even all of these characteristics—sometimes the journalist writes better than we expect. But the script that is envisioned in an "out of time—out of place" atmosphere belongs to the "literary" category and is more likely to live than one dated by events and characters or the demands of a specific audience or that is noted primarily for its effectiveness in production.

MORALITY VS. IMMORALITY

A final word on the script's substance concerns a phase that is often the first to be discussed. We refer to the question of a play's morality.

Long dissertations on artistic freedom or pleas for broadmindedness on the part of the audience are of no avail. What we must establish is a basic and honest measuring stick to enable the intelligent theatregoer to judge what he sees and hears and thus decide for himself. Few would deny our premise that the theatre is a reflection of life. It follows logically that its duty is to picture life truthfully as well as artistically. It must not show just one phase of life or the little segment of which an individual approves but *all* life of *all* classes and *all* groups and *all* personalities and *all* ages. We do not necessarily agree with the man who said: "Good plays are only written about bad people." We do contend that if some evil does not appear to conflict or contrast with the good, it cannot be a very satisfactory play. It is *only* when the supposed evil succeeds, or is praised for its own sake, that the play might be open to the criticism of being immoral.

In some of our more conservative areas it is the minor sins, such as using the Lord's name in vain, excessive drinking or drug-taking, or a suggestion of sex deviation or promiscuity, that bring forth the first charge of immorality. Like the proverbial ostrich, this small segment of the populace bury their heads in the sand and close their eyes to the things they do not want to see. Judging the world by their personal codes of morality, they rate themselves as above reproach and frown upon any different personal conduct.

No so-called sins need be endorsed, but all types of behavior should be recognized as existing in life, and if the artist is to portray life, he needs to include them. If the character is a profane man or a drinking man, it is more moral and honest to picture him thus than to falsely alter his character. The audience need only remember that the playwright is describing a particular character, not all men; they should see and understand *that* character as an individual. In short, it is the obligation of the audience *to judge the characters of a play in terms of life, rather than to judge life in terms of a particular play or character.*

Ibsen does not say that all women should leave their husbands, but that Nora—one woman, who is not permitted to be an adult, to have a personality, or to live a life of her own—does have the right to walk out of her home and leave her family. Ibsen wrote in a day when the double standard was generally accepted. He challenged that belief, along with many other conventional ideas of his period.

So long as the author has a true insight into the lives of his characters and pictures them as they are, the play is moral. If he makes his audience admire a vile character or invents excuses for situations that have no valid excuses, lauds the villainy within them, allows weakness to be rewarded, or lies in any way about his characters, then he may leave himself open to the charge of immorality.

The whole question of morality is as involved as human nature itself, but the basis for determining morality in the theatre should be one of honest and objective analysis. With this fundamental principle in mind we may ask some specific questions:

Has the playwright lied about his characters? If at any point he has, the play, by our standards, is immoral.

Has the author permitted any evil or wrong to be rewarded? Have the wicked achieved their goals because of or through their wickedness? If so, the play may be considered immoral.

Regardless of the answers one may give to these two questions, the artistic merits of a play are not necessarily affected by a decision as to the morality or immorality of its substance. Morality is no guarantee of greatness. Historically and critically, the "three S's"—sincerity, style, and simplicity—have been considered of far more importance. These shall be studied further in a discussion of the playwright's form.

FORM IN PLAY-WRITING

TYPES OF PLAY

Though Polonius, in humoring Hamlet, listed the types of drama as "tragedy, comedy, history, pastoral, pastoral-comical, historical-pastoral, tragical-historical, tragical-comical-historical-pastoral," we have, for many years, been satisfied with four general classifications. If the subject of the play were a serious one, it might be tragedy or melodrama; if of a lighter nature, comedy or farce. Gradually the lines between these categories have become blurred. As tragedy became more difficult to write because of our scientific discoveries and man's inability to determine his own ends, there arose in France the "drame," which was serious but neither tragedy nor melodrama. In America we sometimes settled for "drama," and Mr. Gassner frequently referred to a play as being "in the foothills of tragedy." Today the avant-garde playwrights, especially Ionesco, have given us a type that can best be called "tragi-farce." We shall speak more of this in our consideration of the avant-garde.

The discussions that follow should be considered as primarily applicable to the conventional drama and even then they should never be thought of as absolute. In the past half-century there has been more and more mingling of the serious with the comic, with less importance given to both plot and story. This has made it increasingly difficult to classify a play as to its type or genre. The following discussions, however, can be of value in understanding this area of the playwright's form.

The "requirements" listed for each of the four general types are arbitrary and change with the years. Debatable as they may be today, they have grown out of what are considered the very best of the various types in dramatic literature.

Tragedy

Tragedy is the oldest type of written drama, and has always been based on certain assumptions:

The full reality of the Ego.

The supreme importance of man in the universe, where he is only a little below the gods.

The responsibility of man for his own conduct.

Tragedy has always been of a serious nature and is ranked as one of the most artistic endeavors of civilized man. Tragedies have presented the spectacle of a great or noble human being shattering himself against insuperable obstacles because he will not compromise with circumstances or conditions as they exist. The Greeks were in conflict with the gods, the Elizabethans with some fault within themselves, and the moderns have found their conflict in their surroundings, but always the force is greater than the individual, and he must go down in defeat. The leading character, or "protagonist," has until recent times been a person of high station or an individual with some nobility. In more modern plays he has been a representative of a class or a social group.

Two specific emotions experienced by an audience in great tragedy are pity and fear—pity for those who seem to be suffering unjustly, and fear that the same circumstances could apply to them.

The very essence of tragedy is metaphysical—an inquiry into the nature of our very existence. It goes beyond the material or the physical as the protagonist confronts the mysteries of his being in the circumstances with which he is faced. It recognizes the darkest side of our existence—the uncertainties of meaning and purpose. The issues raised cannot be settled logically or rationally. Tragedy shows man himself as a paradox in a paradoxical situation: he is pictured as both fallible and vulnerable—yet capable of greatness. He may freely use his will to accomplish his ends, but he still is the plaything of destiny. The final paradox in the tragic vision says: "I do not believe that evil is invincible, but I can only see that defeat is inevitable."

Why this is so is the question all tragedy asks and no tragedy answers, even though the tragic hero triumphs in his defeat. This is what Aristotle calls "wisdom through suffering" or "beauty in ugliness" or "purgation of the emotions" or "catharsis." It is the recognition by the tragic hero of what is happening to him—a knowledge that he is not perfect and, therefore, responsible for his fate. In the area of psycho-analysis it is the elimination of complexes and frustrations by bringing them into consciousness and giving them expression. The leading figure on the stage passes through a great crisis and in that crisis comes to be aware of a personal weakness or fault within himself. He may have lost the battle and his life—but he dies a happier and better man for having recognized his imperfection.

John Gassner called this recognition *enlightenment*—enlightenment of the spirit, even though the body may die. Enlightenment does not mean the acquisition of factual knowledge from the words of the play, or from the action or dialogue, but rather something felt or achieved by the leading character and through him transferred to the audience. Gassner said that pity, fear, and enlightenment thus become a "marriage of emotion and understanding." This feeling must rise above the perturbing events of the play.

We in the audience, with full knowledge of our own frustrations, inhibitions, personal faults, and weaknesses, see those human errors brought out into the open on the stage, and thus we, too, are spiritually cleansed. The play serves as a sort of public confession, but this is not enough in itself. We must put our own houses in order by resolving to go out of the theatre better men or women and to cast these evil elements out of our being.

It is this enlightenment that is so essential to tragedy. Sometimes it happens in the audience and sometimes it is only sensed or recognized by the audience as it occurs within the leading character in the play. It is our own recognition or failure to recognize this enlightenment that causes so much debate over whether much of our modern serious drama is tragedy or melodrama. So much depends on how much we personally relate to it, and this is a result of our background, knowledge, and sensitivity. Some dramas that have created heated discussions over whether or not they had reached the high level of tragedy are *Death of a Salesman, Long Day's Journey into Night, Winterset, Saint Joan, Desire Under the Elms, Blood Wedding,* and *The House of Bernarda Alba.*

In plays written specifically for the screen, rarely have we seen great tragedy. There the temptation to bring in the effects of chance, excitement, and sentimentality have changed the possible tragedies into melodramas—frequently of a high order—but melodramas nevertheless.

If we consider those plays generally accepted as tragedies from all periods, we find there are five basic principles. When a playwright fails to meet *any one* of these demands, he is outside the realm of pure tragedy:

The play must have a serious subject.

The leading character must be a great figure or one who is representative of a class.

The incidents must be absolutely honest and without the element of coincidence or chance. What should happen must happen.

The basic emotions are those of pity and fear—pity for the protagonist in his suffering and fear that the same fate might come to us.

In the final analysis the protagonist must meet defeat, but before that defeat must come enlightenment or the *catharsis* of Aristotle.

Melodrama

Where the tragic writer has said: "What is the one thing these people would do under these circumstances?", the writer of melodrama has said, "What is the most thrilling action I can devise here?", and then, "How can I make it seem logical that the characters would do this?" This often brings about inconsistencies in the characterizations of those involved in the plot. One escapade rapidly follows another, and the excitement that ensues makes melodrama one of the most entertaining and popular types of drama. Most of the serious motion pictures and television plays we see are melodramas, and yet many are so well disguised that a majority of those who see and praise them would be indignant if we suggested that they had seen a melodrama.

Webster defines melodrama as "a kind of drama, commonly romantic and sensational, with both songs and instrumental music interspersed; hence, any romantic and sensational drama, typically with a happy ending." As a form it has existed since the very beginning of the theatre, though in earlier times it may have been called tragicomedy and today is often merely called drama. The term melodrama came into existence in the nineteenth century and grew out of the expression, *drama with music,* for "melodrama" had its origin under those circumstances. The stage later abandoned the music, although motion pictures readopted it as part of their own technique, and as one sees the motion-picture or television melodrama today, with the almost inevitable musical background, he wonders if the cycle may not have completed itself.

Perhaps a word in defense would not be out of place, for the term melodrama unfortunately is very much in disrepute, since in those melo-dramas that came to us in the late nineteenth century—*Uncle Tom's Cabin; Bertha, the Sewing-Machine Girl; The Streets of New York; Ten Nights in a Barroom;* and *East Lynne* to name a few—black was black and white was white. The playwright pitted good against evil, excitement was the key word, and coincidence a commonplace. Because of its connotations many persons feel that to praise a melodrama or to admit a liking for it is a mark of discredit, not realizing that the vast majority of serious plays written in this century fall naturally into this category. Both tragedy and melodrama are legitimate approaches to the planning of a serious play, for in each it is possible to give a truthful representation of life. Life itself is divided between chance and character. Melodrama would make more of the chance; tragedy would place emphasis upon character. Melodrama would show what might happen; tragedy would show what must happen. While tragedy *must tell the truth,* melodrama *must not lie,* and the world knows well that there is a vast difference between those two injunctions. Arthur Miller has said: "When I show you why a man does what he does, I may do it melodramatically; but when I show you why he almost did not do it, I am making drama." In melodrama there is a chance of victory, for the protagonist is the victim of external circumstances over which he may win; tragedy exists when the protagonist *has within him the power to win,* but is, nevertheless, doomed to failure.

Melodramas make for exciting theatre. They can move an audience to tears of sympathy as well as to overt action. They have made great contributions in dramatizing social, economic, and religious questions. It is certainly the common man's most popular serious theatre, for he can easily relate to it. The characters are vivid, and in the twentieth century their psychological motivations are heavily stressed. They are normally completely sympathetic or completely antipathetic. The latter characters usually instigate complications that cause difficulties for the former. As characters, they do not grow or change as in tragedies. After many narrow escapes and much excitement the sympathetic character is saved at the very last moment and wrongs are punished and innocence rewarded, thus bringing about a double ending. Strict moral justice is a cornerstone, and this triumph over evil is popular with the audience.

Pity is the basic emotion, but it is often born of sentimentality, which we define as having an emotion without paying for it with thought or analysis. We sympathize with a child because he is a child or with a pretty girl just because she is pretty and in distress without analyzing the causes. In reality, neither may truly deserve our sympathy. Emotion reigns rather than reason. Life is a conflict between good and bad—often with no in-between. Situations are not analyzed or thought through and human feeling dominates. Favorite stories show different versions of the young man struggling to be honest against the commercially minded world; the innocence of childhood; down-trodden minority groups; the successful struggles of poor but honest persons; motherhood; the rehabilitation of gamblers, gangsters, women of the streets, drunkards, or dope addicts; and the complete reformation of the hard-hearted and stingy old man whose soul is saved through the love of a little child—the formula can be recognized any day on television. Sentimentality is thus an important element of melodrama. There may be fear, but it is of a more temporary or superficial variety. We are more interested in the situation and the circumstances than we are in the intricacies of the characters involved. Sentimentality under control can possess great emotional power; out of control, it only lies.

The characters in melodrama being as inauthentic as they are, the members of the audience are able to fit themselves into any role and thus relate more completely to it. The story seems to deal with charmed lives, for the ending is nearly always a happy one. Herein lies the greatest appeal of melodrama to the average motion-picture, television, and theatre audience. It furnishes them excitement and happiness often denied in their everyday existence, for usually the protagonist wins his struggle.

As in tragedy, there are five principles that can be considered as basic to melodrama:

It treats of a serious subject.

Characters, though loosely drawn for easy audience identification, are clearly defined. Good triumphs and evil is punished—a double ending. Strong empathy is created in the audience.

Whereas tragedy must be absolutely honest, the element of chance enters into the melodrama. It is episodic, and the most exciting incidents possible are brought into the play.

There may be pity, but it borders on sentimentality. Fear may be evident, but it is of a more temporary or superficial type.

There is no real enlightenment even in defeat, and in most instances the protagonist does win his battle.

One can justify a good melodrama as escape or as an artistic theatrical experience. As escape it has great popularity with the masses because it permits them to forget their own problems as they view the troubles of another. There is no strain or suffering on their part. These are the basic reasons for the preponderance of low-grade melodramas on our television and motion-picture screens.

As an artistic theatrical experience it can present truths or themes from which we and society can profit, create an awareness of injustice and human needs or errors that can be remedied, and clarify our thinking on personal problems and give us courage for living, though it does fall short of possessing the true catharsis of tragedy.

As critics we should evaluate each type in its own realm of theatrical entertainment, for each should be accepted as a wholly legitimate means of relating a serious story.

The Areas of Comedy

Man is the only animal on the face of the earth capable of realizing the miseries of life and the only one who possesses the God-given privilege of knowing how to laugh. This may be due to the fact that all the other animals were created before man and therefore had nothing to laugh at!

Comedy is only a point of view. The very seed of comedy lies in the intellect—in our ability to think rather than to feel—to stand outside a situation and see it in perspective. Who of us is there who cannot remember countless incidents in the past about which we permitted ourselves to become so emotionally concerned that they took on the significance of a real crisis, yet today we look back and laugh at both the incident and ourselves. True comedy is oftentimes tragedy plus time or distance.

All comedy—whether it be burlesque, buffoonery, wit, humor, satire, parody, or criticism—belongs in the top drawer of the intellect, and in a world made up entirely of intelligence it is possible that there would be very few tears, but there would always be laughter. It was Hugh Walpole who said that "life is a comedy to those who think and a tragedy to those who feel." Max Beerbohm contended that "only the emotion of love was on a higher level than the emotion of laughter."

The very heart of comedy lies in our recognition of how far our fellow man has fallen from the ideal. It is measured by the sharpness of our perception in recognizing those differences between what man is and what he tries or pretends to be. Comedy is the sworn enemy of hypocrisy and pretense and would tear away all the falderal, the paint and powder, the sham, the military medals, and the college degrees and show that at the very foundation, the great hero is just like everyone else. Comedy is God's gift to disinfect the world of pomposity.

Though we may laugh at both wit and humor, there is a vast difference between the two. Wit is of the head, while humor is of the head and the heart. Wit laughs *at* people, while humor laughs *with* people as they laugh at themselves, at their own foibles and at their own fancies. Wit plays practical jokes, ridicules, makes fun, but humor knows no contempt. Humor is the very essence of love; it loves people and loves seeing people enjoy themselves. The laughter of humor is a laughter of kindness, of gentleness, of companionship and understanding that pulls mankind together in one happy family of fellow fools and sinners. The root of our finest humor lies in character. It was E. B. White who once said: "Real humor comes very close to that great big hot fire of truth, and sometimes the viewer feels the heat." More than a hundred years earlier Goethe had written: "The only time that man recognizes himself is when he sees himself in others." Seeing oneself in the humorous antics of another is positive proof of a true sense of humor—which is in itself a safety valve that can protect man from the tensions and frustrations of everyday life.

The Greeks sought their catharsis in tragedy. In our time we believe that comedy can do it equally well—that nothing so completely cleanses and clears the mind and the spirit as unadulterated laughter. *Time* magazine once printed a two-page article on the subject of humor that ended with the statement: "One thing that the United States can always use is something that everyone has within him—a good laugh."

We should be eternally grateful for comedy and for laughter. Of all the gifts God gave to man, one of the rarest, one of the subtlest, and one of the most precious is laughter. It knows no religion, no politics, no nationality. As an equalizer it has no equal. We all laugh in the same language.

Farce	*High Comedy*
	6. Comedy of ideas and satire
	5. Inconsistencies of character
	4. Verbal wit
	3. Plot devices
	2. Physical mishaps
1. Obscenity	

Our system for recognizing the elements or areas of comedy has been given us by Alan Reynolds Thompson.* His "ladder of comedy" is our clearest picture of this subject. If studied carefully it can be most helpful in differentiating between the two types of humor—comedy and farce.

* Alan Reynolds Thompson, *The Anatomy of the Drama* (Berkeley: University of California Press, 1946). Reprinted by permission of the Regents of the University of California.

The reader must never forget, however, that the artist's treatment of the material will determine whether it is high farce that borders on comedy, or low comedy that borders on farce. This does not imply that one is any better than the other; each is a legitimate method of presenting a lighter story.

Obscenity in humor is considered the lowest form of comedy. It needed little explanation until recently, for it was very scarce in our theatre, except when combined with one of the higher forms of humor as a necessary part of a specific character or situation. There were times in dramatic literature when the digestive processes and the most animalistic elements of love-making were common in many stage productions. The audience expected and accepted these as a logical part of the play. The phallus, as a symbol of fertility, was usually present in Greek comedy. The repartee of the Restoration period (1660–1725) would have shocked almost any theatre audience from that time until the mid-twentieth century. Profanity, though it has always been a problem with the community and educational theatre, has been pretty well accepted in the commercial theatre since the advent of *What Price Glory?* soon after World War I. Nudity, however, was principally relegated to the burlesque houses until the first nude scene in *Hair* in the mid-sixties. Since that time it has become a kind of obligatory scene in many plays. If nudity is part of the play's purpose or meaning it can have validity. The obscenity charge arises validly when it is used only for shock or publicity value. Ironically, the whole matter of nudity seems to possess a kind of national significance. Every famous art museum in the Western world prides itself on its nude figures of both sexes—in its statuary and its paintings. At the same time, some who praise this art are shocked by nudity in the theatre. It is the reverse in the Orient. One never sees a nude figure in any work of art, but in life communal bathing or swimming in the nude is wholly accepted. During the occupation, the Japanese people found it difficult to understand the American soldier's delight in a strip-tease performance.

Obscenity today is difficult to classify. The generation gap, the matter of personal taste, the variety of intelligence in analyzing its use or its necessity—all force each of us to view it differently.

Moving up the ladder of comedy, we come to *physical mishap*. The most obvious example is the common pratfall: jerking a chair out from under an unsuspecting character, a banana peel that sends someone sprawling across the stage, the custard pie thrown in the face, the dignified man or woman caught in the stream of water from a hose. Much of what is called slapstick comedy comes under this category. These physical elements are found today only in the broadest of comedy or in an occasional motion-picture or television farce. When they do appear, the discerning critic cannot refrain from exclaiming: "Oh, no, no, not that, please!" for the distinction is so fine between farce, which we must believe, and burlesque, which we need not believe, that it takes a real artist to know and to keep within these boundaries.

The third step is *plot device*. Shakespeare, whose comedies are rarely considered on a par with his tragedies, often turned to this type of comedy and did it most effectively. It involves misunderstandings, cross purposes, inopportune or embarrassing occurrences, mistaken identity, and so on. In this area of comedy the author manipulates the characters and situations into hilarious combinations and ludicrous situations.

The next step is *verbal wit*. Even in reading, the dialogue will seem humorous and in production can send an audience into gales of laughter. In the English language few playwrights have surpassed Oscar Wilde's great gift for this sort of comedy. He is known for such epigrams as these: "To love oneself is the beginning of a lifelong romance"; "Wicked women bother one. Good women bore one. That is the only difference between them"; "There's nothing in the world like the devotion of a married woman. It's a thing no married man knows anything about"; "Experience is the name everybody gives to their mistakes"; and one as modern as "Spies are of no use nowadays. The newspapers do their work instead." His *The Importance of Being Earnest* is considered our most perfect example of verbal wit. In the English language verbal wit, or linguistic comedy as it is sometimes called, goes back to Shakespeare, with characters like Dogberry and Bottom who are mastered *by* the language—and amuse with what have become known as malapropisms—and characters like Beatrice and Benedict who master the language. George Bernard Shaw and Noel Coward carry verbal wit into the twentieth century. Linguistic comedy includes punning, which in the hands of Shakespeare or James Joyce can be masterful.

In America, George S. Kaufman, Moss Hart, and Neil Simon are known for their wit. They frequently handle the characters who will speak the lines in such a way that the distinction between farce and comedy is difficult to make.

Obscenity, physical mishap, plot device (or situation), and verbal wit (or linguistic comedy)—these four elements of comedy are considered the basic materials of farce. The fact that they are ranked low on the ladder of comedy does not mean that they should be considered any less artistic. A study of most of the examples would reveal that the authors were able *by their treatment* to lift the farcical material to a high degree of artistry—even as farce, which can always be a legitimate part of comedy. We could point out many plays that failed because the farcical material received inadequate treatment and the plays were for that reason undistinguished. It is important that we be able to recognize the material itself and also the nature of the treatment it has received by the artist. These may be separate entities.

Character is the foundation of comedy and *inconsistency* of character is our next step in the ladder of comedy. Here the unexpected on the part of an individual is found in the surprise action or speech that is so contrary to his appearance or nature and yet is believable as a characteristic rather than simply as a humorous touch. Inconsistency may also be found in a discrepancy between professed and real qualities in a character. As Henry Fielding said in his preface to *Joseph Andrews*, the only source of the true ridiculous is affectation, which proceeds from one of two causes, vanity and hypocrisy, and this accounts for the majority of comic characters.

In the theatre, as in life, man has attained the pinnacle of humor when he reaches what Mr. Thompson has called a *comedy of ideas*, or *satire*. These qualities of humor are found in man's ability to laugh at that which is closest to his heart—his family, his friends, his religion, his politics, his country, himself. It is a gift of irreverence—an ability to be amused by the things we take seriously. One possesses a real sense of humor when one can recognize and appraise one's own pretensions and shortcomings. This is sometimes called high comedy and may be defined as a criticism of life, though we repeat that farce, too, by its treatment can be raised to the level of satire. Sometimes the laughter is violent and angry, and sometimes delightful, tongue-in-cheek, accompanied by the awareness of an intensity of purpose, because both the characters involved and we as an audience realize the seriousness of their acts and thoughts as well as the humor involved in them.

The very proximity of farce to comedy in the realm of humor is exemplified by the common denominator of the highest comedy and the lowest farcical material: they both demand a sense of detachment on the part of the audience. Both frown upon sentiment and sentimentality, and neither will tolerate the audience's identifying itself with what it sees on the stage. There must be perspective—aesthetic distance—in comedy. Both high comedy and farce regard life objectively, and either can work toward the elimination of social injustice or the individual's flaws in his own personal habits. As Molière has wisely said: "People do not mind being wicked, but they object to being made ridiculous."

We would emphasize once more that even though Mr. Thompson's ladder indicates that farce and comedy materials belong to different levels, the highest of comedy can be made to appear the lowest of farce, and the most blatant farce can, by its treatment, be lifted into the upper realm of comedy. This is to say that nothing in itself must be either one or the other, but that the treatment of the artist may make the material one or the other.

The diagram and discussion will bear careful study and analysis, for if they are understood they can be of great assistance in our effort to distinguish between comedy and farce.

Comedy

Comedy is the most miscellaneous of all the dramatic forms and therefore the most difficult to define. There are people who measure a given play against the requirements of tragedy, melodrama, or farce, and when it has failed to meet any of these, call it comedy. We know that it must present believable and understandable characters, that the situations should be both possible and probable, that it should treat of the individual and his personal problems, and that it should concern the lighter side of life. While a comedy may often use a serious subject as its substance, such as infidelity, war, communism, tolerance, religion, marriage, or divorce, it does treat that subject more lightly than does melodrama. In comedy the protagonist has within him the power to alter the immediate obstacle.

Much of comedy is based on incidents that, occurring in the life of others, provoke laughter in us, but happening to us, would be found unpleasant. It is the element of perspective that gives us the detachment we need. The seriousness with which the characters involved attack the problem provokes us to laughter.

In comedy the protagonist usually overcomes his obstacles, but the means by which he gains success should be consistent with the laws of life. We may, as an audience, laugh at the situations even while we sympathize with the characters.

A common and mistaken belief is that comedies must have a happy ending. The conclusion must be honest and in the spirit of the play, but need not be a happy one.

Historically, the Greeks reveled in a rollicking sort of humor with much biting satire. The Romans leaned toward buffoonery and ingenious plots. The Elizabethans gave us the romantic comedy of Shakespeare, with its lyrical poetry and light-hearted stories of love and adventure. In addition, there was the comedy of Ben Jonson, with bitter satire and ridicule of the man in the street.

Molière is considered to be the greatest writer of comedy who has ever lived. His was the most skillful satire, and his plays are said to have evoked the "thoughtful laughter" which is the final and true test of comedy. This is in contrast to the "thoughtless laughter" brought forth by the farcical elements described in the following section. Various names (*comedy of manners, high comedy, artificial comedy,* and *intellectual comedy*) have been given this kind of comedy, whose purpose it is to satirize the social customs of the upper classes. There is also a *serious* or *sentimental comedy* label for those scripts that may touch our sympathy and our emotions very deeply while they provoke a thoughtful evaluation of the characters' predicament.

No one would question that comedy is one of the most popular of all types, being challenged only by farce. If man wants escape he can usually find it through laughter, and too often he cares not how it is provoked.

This brief description of what comedies have included and do include, plus the differentiation that preceded, should now make it possible to draw up some basic tests for comedy. A survey of the best comedies in twenty-five hundred years of theatre shows that comedy:

Treats its subject in a lighter vein even though the subject may be a serious one.

Provokes what can be defined as "thoughtful laughter."

Is both possible and probable.

Grows out of character rather than situation.

Is honest in its portrayal of life.

Farce

Use of the word *comedy* while thinking in terms of *farce* is a common error. Farce is to comedy what melodrama is to tragedy. It consists of exaggerated incidents and characters, with a domination of plot and only a pretense of reality. More often than not it develops through a series of misunderstandings between the characters involved. The generalization is still true that comedy is both possible and probable, while farce is possible, but not very probable. Farce has been called a purely mathematical sequence of laughs in which the object of the author is to make the audience believe only for the moment. The incidents come rapidly, and the whole play is episodic. The audience is given little time to think, because farce portrays the strictly ludicrous in life; if the spectators did analyze the action, believability would be sacrificed. Farce depends upon extreme improbability that usually grows out of someone's mental or physical distress. It is a paradox that this type of humor has always flourished most in ages of great cultural activity and refinement. The reason lies in the fact that farce, though improbable, is usually based on logic and objectivity, qualities which are an integral part of education and culture.

The author of a farce usually asks the audience to grant him a few improbabilities at the very beginning, but from this point on he proceeds in a world of reality. It is often true that a farce exists when the whole story would evaporate and the play be concluded if at any time each character were to tell the whole truth. However, it is our acceptance of this opening improbability or this lack of knowledge common to all the characters that makes the series of events so highly enjoyable.

While observing a farce in production we should, with a modicum of "imaginary puissance," believe what we are watching. We may not believe the story or the characters once out of the theatre, and perhaps not even during the intermissions, but while the actual performance is on there must be a sense of believability—at least to a detached, fairy-story degree.

For almost a century one of our most famous farces has been *Charley's Aunt*, which Ray Bolger made into the very popular musical comedy *Where's Charley?* As a stage piece this has had one of the most amazing careers. Ludicrous as it is in content, an audience is ready to accept the improbabilities and howl with laughter with temporary be-lief—*if* the players attack these improbable situations with sincerity—because it is so theatrically effective. Measured by the tests that follow, this play becomes an almost perfect example of farce.

The dialogue of farce may run from the epigram of Oscar Wilde to the "gag" in the most recent television script. In either instance any speech could be given to almost any character in the play, for the lines have no special relationship to character but exist for the laugh value they possess in themselves. We can see the logic of this fact when we realize that the term *farce* comes to us from the Latin word meaning "to stuff."

Like melodrama, a well produced farce is most delightful. Both motion pictures and television lean heavily upon this type and in it have done some of their most superior work.

The qualities of farce that have been most constant through the ages are that it:

Has as its object riotous laughter and escape.

Asks the audience to accept certain improbabilities but from that point proceeds in a life-like manner.

Is possible but not very probable.

Is dominated by situation rather than character and calls for little or no thought.

Must move rapidly in an episodic manner and is believable only for the moment.

STYLE—PERSONAL AND AESTHETIC

We define style as the sum of all those qualities that differentiate a work of art from reality. The artist takes his material from life as he sees it. He then presents that material as art. In the transition he must see that nothing is left out that is essential and nothing is added that does not contribute to the total effect. He gives it balance, proportion, and grace as he integrates the many parts and creates a complete unity. Style, more than any other single quality, distinguishes an artist or his work. It is evident when substance and form achieve their final excellence. Joseph Wood Krutch once described it as: "Style—that indefinable kind of magic that distinguishes a personality and makes a person original—different—memorable." In this sense we must always think of style as possessing two qualities, the personal and the aesthetic.

First there is the personal style of the artist, which many would prefer to call his technique. It involves the spirit of the script or the production and represents each artist's individual touch. It is how he views the whole situation, whether he chooses to imitate life or to suggest it, and the particular choices he may elect to emphasize in that imitation or suggestion. It is how he will tell the story, the shadings he will give the dialogue—regardless of the particular aesthetic style he may have used. A good example of personal style is found in music. The same selection may be performed by countless singers or orchestras, but each interpretation is peculiarly the work of a particular person or group. Impressionists, in giving their imitations of prominent personalities, must catch and imitate the personal style of their subjects. An avid play reader is aware of this in the playwright's work after reading only a few speeches from his latest work. The same is true in a novel or poem. It is the artist's personal style that raises or lowers the various steps of comedy material discussed under the ladder of comedy.

Once the dramatist begins his work he becomes involved in what we call the aesthetic style. First there was the classic style, which grew out of the open-air Greek theatres; then came the romantic, of which Shakespeare is considered the greatest practitioner, at least in the English-speaking world; and finally the realistic, with which we are most familiar in our modern theatre. Less used, but important, are symbolism, which is sometimes found mixed with one of the other styles; expressionism, which was an effort to break away from the ultra-realistic; and, today, the surrealistic style of the avant-garde. Fantasy is frequently considered a style in itself, though usually combined with another style; this is a fairy-tale quality, highly imaginative, and concerned with events and characters far from reality, but wholly true in that imagined world.

We shall now consider some of the specific attributes of the most prominent aesthetic styles.

Theatricalism

This has been discussed in chapter 1 as a basic assumption in theatre. Oftentimes it may either predominate or stand alone as a style. It is nearly always present in the treatment of or in combination with one of the other aesthetic styles.

Classicism

In the classic style there is a certain worship of form and orderliness. Choruses usually give us the necessary information or background; the dialogue is often in verse; one mood predominates—comedy is not found next to tragedy in the same play; and there is a loftiness, dignity, and distance on the part of the characters involved.

Romanticism

The romantic style is more indifferent to form and order. It disregards tradition and scorns the practical everyday life. Time may be telescoped; all is on a plane of imaginative grandeur. The idealistic or imaginative is always present. The characters live what seem to be charmed lives in a world of theatre rather than a world of reality. Existence is filled with excitement, suspense, success. The locale is some faraway or fictitious place; the playwright is unhampered in the placement of his action or in the choice of characters. He may choose prose or verse or silence, but he writes with a freedom, a beauty of language, and an imagination that permits his characters to do and feel what we would like to think is possible.

Realism

A frequent criticism by the untutored is that any play not using the language with which we are all so familiar is "unnatural" or "unreal." This criticism, of course, rises from a basic misunderstanding of the words *reality* and *realism*. Reality is life itself. The only reality that is possible in the theatre is in the mind of the spectator—the stage has none. It can only present an approximation of reality, for every part of a dramatic performance is a conscious stylization or imitation. "Realism" is the term used to denote the artist's aesthetic style in portraying that reality. It is his interpretation of reality and is composed of his selection and arrangement. It stresses the practical, everyday details of our existence and pictures the ugliness as well as the beauty. Man's most intimate problems are discussed, and the characters speak like those we might meet in our daily lives. Time is accounted for. An individual character's motives and actions must meet the tests of modern psychology. This is the style that was introduced by Henrik Ibsen, and it has dominated our theatre for almost one hundred years. It finds its forte in the motion pictures and to an even greater degree in television productions.

Expressionism

Expressionism, like symbolism, represents an effort to move away from realism or the portrayal of surface meaning. It is considered to have begun in Germany, reaching its peak there shortly after World War I, although its real source is in the dream plays of August Strindberg (1849–1912). Its purpose was to show man's inner self as well as his outer person, contending that the inner man is a truer "reality" than the outer one that the world sees and knows. In expressionistic plays the dramatist tries to find a means of exposing the inner man. *Death of a Salesman* is a happy combination of the realistic and the expressionistic styles as stark reality is pictured in one scene while the thoughts that existed in the mind of Willy Loman are enacted almost simultaneously. Expressionism does not always put scenes in chronological order; the grotesque is often present; there is much emphasis on mood, distortion, and frustration. The work is highly imaginative, and the production must project the same spirit. Because its chief effort is to broaden the realistic theatre, expressionism always attempts to suggest far more of life than it portrays.

Surrealism

This style came into existence shortly before 1920 and grew out of Dadaism, known for its meaninglessness. The Dadaists were basically negative and elevated the irrational and illogical to a position of primary importance. Their style is now considered a fad. It gave way to surrealism, which, although it peaked in the 1920s, has been reactivated by the absurdists. It looks upon the principal source of truth as the subconscious mind, whose greatest strength is in dreams when the mind is free from rational control. (Here it borrows much from Strindberg and expressionism.) It views the world as essentially irrational and, though until recently it has produced no dramas of merit, it has been the forerunner of other schools and because of its importance in the theatre of the absurd we must consider it here.

Epic

The *Epic Style* was introduced by Bertolt Brecht (1898–1956), a Marxist who felt the theatre should not waste its time with make-believe, but rather had a duty to change the world. Brecht chose the word *epic* to distinguish his work from the more conventional and dramatic theatre. He was always an anti-Aristotelian, rebelling principally against the "illusion and the empathy that have been so great a part of the

Western theatre." Although epic drama is imitative to a certain point, Brecht was violently opposed to an audience becoming too involved with what they witnessed. He wanted them to realize that the injustices being portrayed existed all about them. As an advocate of social reform, Brecht wanted the audience to do something about these unsavory situations.

In seeking the effect he desired of preventing the audience from becoming involved emotionally with the illusion on stage, he introduced the word *verfremdung,* which has been translated as "alienation." We prefer the alternate translation, "estrangement," for this comes much closer to what Brecht did in practice.

The goal of epic theatre is to break up the emotion and to make the audience always aware that they are in the theatre. For example, light or fantastic music is often used as a background for a very somber scene. In theory, there is opposition to illusion or to an audience becoming involved in the play. Brecht's ideal audience should be emotionally moved, but their experienced emotions should stimulate action when the play is ended. This style will be further discussed on pp. 70–74.

The Absurd

The most recent revolt against both the realistic and the epic style is the *absurd.* While epic theatre presents a message, the absurd finds communication either impossible or hardly worthwhile. It emphasizes interruption, incongruity, senseless logic, and constant repetition. It borrows much from expressionism, but goes even further in its obscurity and pessimism as it expands on the disintegration of the psyche and the breakdown of all personal relationships. This whole movement will be further discussed in the section on avant-garde theatre.

Symbolism~Fantasy

Symbolism tells two stories at once in that what we see or hear recalls a parallel situation or emotion. *Fantasy* is thoroughly imaginative and embodies purely hypothetical or fairy-story situations. Most of Walt Disney's work is in the realm of fantasy; an occasional motion picture is in this style, and many television scripts have used it successfully.

An effect of some reality may be found in any aesthetic style. Fantasy, romanticism, classicism, absurdism may be just as real as the most obvious realism. In the more imaginative world of the Greek theatre or that of Shakespeare or of the writers of fantasy, the characters are just as real and just as natural, but in terms of their own world. They are characters of a fictional reality and as such are more likely to live for future generations than are the realistic characters of our modern drama.

Hamlet, Macbeth, Romeo, Oedipus, Antigone, and Electra are less likely to become dated than are the characters in last night's television production or the most recent Broadway success. It is only necessary that the characters live and speak in the reality of their imagined world, that the playwright be consistent with the aesthetic style he has selected, whether he is suggesting or imitating life. There are many who would prefer the purely realistic style. The average theatregoer may find it easier to empathize with the characters in a realistic piece, for what they do comes closer to his own experience. Someone once said: "We must pay for what we get, and we always get just what we pay for." What we have paid for our realism has been an overall littleness of conception, language, and character. It is this "littleness" that has created the demand for greater breadth and depth. The present dramatic revolution is an attempt to answer this demand.

TECHNIQUE IN PLAYWRITING

A playwright does not sit down and analyze the principles that will determine the type or style of his play. His substance, as well as its treatment, will depend on his nature, background, personality, philosophy, knowledge, and experience. The sum total of this treatment—this harmonizing of substance and form—we call his technique or personal style. As we have shown, it may be serious or comedic (type); he may imitate or suggest (style); but he must find just the right atmosphere or mood, the right theatricality, pace, or movement through which he can best project his attitude, message, situation, or character. We turn now to the construction of his script.

STRUCTURE

Since play-writing began with the first script by Aeschylus there have been certain attributes that every play must have. Somehow the audience must be able to know who these characters are that they are observing, what their relationship is to each other, what each desires, and what has happened before we met them. Something must occur to disturb things as they are, to create action, to capture our interest. Once underway, that action must contain some kind of suspense—some surprises or reversals that we would not expect. There must be new information—change or growth in either the characters or the situation or both. Eventually what we see must reach a peak. Usually the issue, whatever it is, is resolved. Although this resolution may not be required, there must be a conclusion of some kind. These elements, in one form or another, have always been present in the making of a play—until the current theatre revolution, when they have often been greatly reduced in importance and sometimes eliminated.

Historically, it remained for the Frenchman, Eugène Scribe (1791–1861) to summarize these common attributes in a simple list of "musts" for the structure of a play. These included:

A clear exposition of situation and characters.

Careful preparation for all that is to occur.

Many unexpected but logical reversals.

Continuous and mounting suspense.

A big scene that was anticipated from the very beginning.

A logical and believable resolution.

Scribe had but one ambition—to entertain the masses. From 1815 to 1861 he did just that, writing or collaborating on some five hundred plays and winning a fantastic popularity throughout the Western world. He most skillfully presented the attitudes and prejudices of the day, but in all his plays he was most careful to retain the *status quo* morally, socially, and politically. His weakness lay in shallowness, for he sacrificed a depth of characterization to plot and intrigue. In 1868 Alexandre Dumas *fils* wrote: "The dramatist who knows *man* as Balzac did and the *theatre* as Scribe did, will be the greatest of the world's dramatists."

It remained for Scribe's student, Victorien Sardou (1831–1908), a more logical-minded man, to put his requirements into a formula, and it is these two men whom we credit with what has come to be known as the "well-made play." Sardou's formula was:

Exposition

Inciting Moment

Rising Action

Turning Point

Falling Action

Climax and Denouement

Conclusion

It is a good exercise to apply this formula to almost any more or less conventional play written since 1860.

The *exposition* usually is found in the first few minutes of the play, for this is where we learn who the characters are, what has happened before we meet them, what they plan to do, and their relationships and feelings toward each other. Suddenly something occurs that disturbs their world as we have found it. This event happens at the *inciting moment*, and when it occurs we know at once what the play is going to be about or what the actors want to bring into reality. The *rising action* is the next phase of the play, in which we see the various forces in conflict, each striving for its own end. This continues until one force seems suddenly to get the advantage over the other; that moment or situation is called the *turning point*. The *falling action* (which is a misnomer, for the interest of the audience must not fall) continues to build the intensity as some new factor enters the picture, and this added element leads to the *climax*, which is the final culmination of everything that has been said and done. The climax pulls all the threads together, and is part of or quickly followed by the *denouement* as the French call it (in translation, the unraveling). Finally there is the *conclusion*, which establishes once more, at least for the moment, the status quo, so that we may leave the theatre with some feeling that this situation has been resolved or at least run its course.

A so-called "well-made play" is the play that follows this strategy as if it were a principle. In such a mechanical script the playwright has failed in both his form and technique. Sometimes the exposition is stretched throughout the entire play and it is possible for the turning point and climax to be almost the same, but something should occur early in act one to disturb the equilibrium if the action is to get underway. Similarly, the tension must build logically to some high point of interest. It has been said that in a three-act play the first act establishes a situation, the second complicates it, and the third resolves it. Few scripts are that simple. A common criticism of television writers is that they leave out the third act. To set up and to complicate a situation is easier than to resolve it. The necessity of rushing into production and the shorter time allowed for presentation are the causes of this weakness.

The well-made play was dealt its most severe blow by Bernard Shaw, who referred to it as "Sardoodledum," and since that time the term "well-made play" has had a derogatory connotation. This is, in one sense, an unfortunate term, for who would deny that a play should be well made?

It has been said that Ibsen added meaning to and put meat on the skeleton of the well-made play and that Shaw put brains in its head. Be that as it may, the formula has persisted in some modified form to the present time, and almost every playwright has used it in his own way. In our current theatre, both structure and the realistic style have suffered in their importance without really losing their inherent power when artistically and appropriately used.

There are some basic factors essential to dramatic structure. They are: emotion, dramatic action, discovery, and change. These should grow out of story, conflict, surprise, crisis, turning point, and climax. There was a heated debate about the relative importance of conflict *versus* crisis in the late nineteenth century. Henry Arthur Jones (1851–1929) seemed to reconcile the two views with his "Universal Law of the Drama," which said:

> Drama arises when any person or persons in a play are consciously or unconsciously "up against" some antagonistic person or circumstance, or fortune. It is often more intense, when as in *Oedipus*, the audience is aware of the obstacle, and the person himself or persons on the stage are unaware of it. Drama arises thus, and continues when or till the person or persons are aware of the obstacle; it is sustained so long as we watch the reaction—physical, mental, or spiritual—of the person or persons to the opposing person, or circumstance, or fortune. It relaxes as this reaction subsides, and ceases when the reaction is complete. This reaction of a person to an obstacle is most arresting and intense when the obstacle takes the form of another human will in almost balanced collision.

Maxwell Anderson (1888–1959) made a valuable contribution when he said:

> A play should lead up to and away from a central crisis, and this crisis should consist in a discovery by the leading character which has an indelible effect on his thought and emotion and completely alters his course of action. The leading character must make the discovery, and it must affect him emotionally, and it must alter his direction in the play.

Two other terms that have created a difference of opinion are *turning point* and *climax*. This has been especially true among those who think of the drama in terms of its literary values as opposed to those who are concerned with its theatrical effectiveness. To the former the terms are often used interchangeably. The latter could choose an interesting analogy from a man's life by using an important event in his early career as the turning point, and for the climax the action or event that ultimately leads to his failure or success:

Turning Point	Climax
A lawyer wins his first case.	He is appointed to the Supreme Court.
A doctor performs his first big operation.	He saves the life of a great personality after others have failed.
A young man turns to drugs or petty larceny.	He commits a crime that sends him to prison for life.
A young man is physically crippled when on the verge of a brilliant career.	He rises above his handicap and makes a great contribution to his country.

STRATEGY AND TACTICS

Further study of the playwright's technique involves what we may call his strategy and his tactics. *Strategy* is the overall plan of the story as the playwright conceives it. The method of carrying out this strategy can be considered his *tactics*, which is the art of weaving in the exposition so that it seems a logical part of the story. He manages to give us all the details about the background and history of the characters and still makes it sound so natural and so much a part of the conversation that it is wholly logical and believable. This is also evident in his ability to create suspense or to bring in the element of surprise. Suspense is the most important single ingredient in any dramatic work and has been defined as that space of time that elapses between an action and its consequences. Expectation is increased and emotion becomes more intense. The ability to hold us off for the very maximum period of time and not strain us is a very important part of an artist's technique. Surprise has a value almost equal to that of suspense, but surprise is not really dramatic unless it fits naturally and logically into the dramatic action. Aside from being sudden and unexpected, it must be relevant to that action; surprise for the sake of surprise is never truly dramatic. A further application of tactics is the manner of getting characters on and off the stage; of giving them sufficient time to accomplish the acts that are necessary to the dramatic action—to motivate their every action and make it logical, meaningful, and in character.

Our great playwrights of the past have been masters in their strategy, in the laying out of an overall plot, but some of them have fallen down on their tactics. On the other hand, our modern playwrights—especially those who have written for the motion pictures and television—have shown great adroitness in the tactics, but frequently have been less successful in their strategy. The observance of the playwright's success in this respect is no small part of our evaluation of his technique.

THEME AND PLOT

The plot has been called the body of a play and the theme has been called its soul. Most plays have a conflict of some kind, which may be between individuals, man and society, man and some superior force, or man and himself. This conflict drives the plot. One of the first items of interest is the playwright's treatment of this plot and the theme he chooses to draw from it. The same plot has been and will be used many times; it is the treatment that makes it different and supplies its originality or artistic worth. Shakespeare is said to have borrowed all but one of his stories from previous authors, but he presented them so much better than had any of the others that he has never been seriously criticized for having done so. The treatment of a theme is equally varied. It would be interesting to count, if one could, the number of television scripts that have proclaimed the theme "crime does not pay" in one way or another.

The same theme or story may be given a very serious or a very light touch. It may be an indictment of mankind or a tongue-in-cheek attack. It could point up a great lesson or show the same situation as a handicap to progress. The personality, background, and social or artistic temperament of the playwright is responsible for the treatment that he gives his story or theme. This we must both understand and evaluate.

Let us imagine how the following playwrights might have treated the simple theme, "today's liberal will be tomorrow's conservative."

Sophocles—who believed that man's character was shaped by the power of self-determination and that the individual was independent of others' opinions.

Shakespeare—who believed character was determined by birth and upbringing, but that man was capable of change under stress if given the choice between right and wrong.

Molière—who contended that man is what he is—no matter what others may think.

Ibsen—who felt no truth lasted more than twenty years and that each individual must constantly evaluate the accepted mores of his day and their effect on his own happiness.

Strindberg—who believed the true reality to lie deep within the subconscious.

Shaw—whose wit and dramatic inversions saw little hope for man ever becoming intelligent enough to answer his problems.

Pirandello—who saw man to be only what others thought him to be; who believed that truth was only relative and rarely the same for any two persons; and who subscribed to the theory of the relativity of dream and reality.

O'Neill—who saw man as the victim of instinct, emotion, and environment in his childlike and rebellious search for identity.

Odets—with his militant drive and enthusiastic charging with all his might.

Maxwell Anderson—who felt that man had lost his capacity to believe in right and wrong as absolutes, and that without this belief a successful life was impossible; and who pursued a mad search for an ethical standard.

Kaufman—with his brilliant wit and constant flow of wisecracks.

Saroyan—with his childlike fantasy and ever-present optimism.

Rice—with his plea for social justice.

Behrman—with his detached, cool, and aloof humor.

Miller—with his dramatic intensity and cry for social liberation.

Sartre—who saw man as his own creator, and who would dismiss both God and past.

Ionesco—with his lucid awareness of life's emptiness, emphasizing anti-logic and lack of communication.

Beckett—with his obsession with death and the monotony of life and its lack of meaning or sense of direction in a hostile universe abandoned by God.

Genet—with his upside down approach to the moral world and his constant use of mirrors and role-playing.

If the dramatist is attempting to tell us something that is not clear, the play does not communicate and is open to criticism on that count. If life is further complicated rather than clarified, the play may have fallen down as a work of art. This does not necessarily mean that we all get the same theme from a given play. Our own backgrounds and our ability to understand may be responsible for our differing with others on the play's full meaning. We may not like the way the playwright has presented his substance or we may question its truth or even cite the dangers inherent in his work, but we should never leave the theatre without knowing what he was trying to say. It is the duty of the playwright, as an artist, to make clear to his audience what he thinks and feels and what he is trying to say or do.

It is, of course, not necessary that the story attempt to teach some great or accepted truth of life, but if it does, the play will have taken on a deeper and more permanent quality. That generally accepted truth is called its theme. Few of us would demand that every play teach a lesson. It is enough for some merely to furnish an escape or amuse the audience for an evening.

If an author chooses to write fluff and smart repartee, he should be given that privilege. If he chooses to write poetic drama, then we should accept the play on its own terms. We need not prefer it or praise it or go to see it, but we should not try to compare the work of the poetic playwright to that of the escapist or the moralist. This was once expressed superbly by Bernard Shaw when he answered a critic who complained that a certain play was not great: "Its author never meant it to be a great play. The question is how does it rank with the type of play it is trying to be?"

To endure, a play should have a theme. It is sometimes suggested in the title, as in *Loyalties, Justice or Strife, You Can't Take It with You,* and *The Doctor in Spite of Himself.* At other times it is found in a speech from the play itself, as in *Craig's Wife,* when the aunt says to Mrs. Craig: "People who live to themselves are often left to themselves." Sometimes it is not so obvious and calls for closer study.

If the author whose desire has been to present a theme has done his job, we should be able to state the theme of his play in general terms and in a single sentence. A possible theme of *Hamlet* could be the failure of a youth of poetic temperament to cope with circumstances that demand action; of *Macbeth,* that too much ambition leads to destruction; of *Streetcar Named Desire,* that he who strives hardest to find happiness oftentimes finds the least; of *Death of a Salesman,* the fallacy of building a life on shallow foundations; and of *Green Pastures,* that even God must change with the universe. Other themes that have been expressed in recent plays are: (1) It is impossible to give away all one's possessions, for even if one gives away the last final shred of his property, he still has the memories of the happiness he has brought to others; (2) one must come very close to death before he really knows how to appreciate life; (3) justice may be turned into a force producing evil as well as good, and human beings, in their weakness, often exploit justice to satisfy selfish aims; (4) evil ever rebounds on the doer, which may be only a more specific statement of the theme expressed in hundreds of scripts that "crime does not pay"; and (5) man is just as good as those who know him believe him to be.

The statement of the play in specific terms is the plot or story that the play presents. Plot and theme should go hand in hand. If the theme is one of nobility or dignity, the plot itself must concern events and characters that measure up to that theme. As we analyze many plays, we find that some possess an excellent theme but are supported by an inconsequential plot. A famous play of this nature was *Abie's Irish Rose* which held the stage for many years. The theme stated that religion is no hindrance to a happy marriage. The plot was so thin and both characters and situations so stereotyped that nothing measured up to the theme. This weakness was most obvious in the play's revival after twenty years.

Examples of the more frequent fault of superior plot and little or no theme come to us in much of the work of our current playwrights. They are known for their cleverness in making the apt remark at the right moment. They are original and extremely witty in their conception, and their plays are very successful with a large following, but more often than not they are utterly lacking in a theme or truth that will withstand more than momentary analysis. They are delightful but ephemeral. An audience believes them only while watching in the theatre. Consequently these authors, although among our most popular, will not endure as artists nor are their plays likely to be revived in the future. They illustrate clearly the axiom that a good plot or conflict is needed for transitory success, but a theme is more likely to assure a play long life.

The greatest single criticism of the conventional theatre is that our playwrights speak well, but far too often have nothing to say. They lack purpose and are given to skimming over the surface, not really getting at the heart of the question. This objection has come from both the right and the left. It is the left—or the avant-garde—that is making the greatest effort to remedy this situation. We shall now consider this very important minority of the current theatre.

THE THEATRE OF THE AVANT-GARDE

The word *avant-garde* comes to us from the French and is a military term. The English translation would be "vanguard," which Webster defines as "the part of an army which goes ahead of the main body in an advance—the leading position in a movement." The avant-garde in literature usually makes its appearance during a period of great stress or turmoil—social, political, religious, or philosophical—and the mid-twentieth century seems to have furnished the perfect soil for its emergence.

We turn now to that vanguard, those who, in this century, have sought to change the conventional, psychological–thesis–problem–realistic theatre into something they have considered more vital and meaningful. These new voices deny that the older forms are capable of expressing reality. They present their substance by disregarding the accepted forms and by using a technique so foreign that the conventional playgoer is often left in a state of amazed wonder. They are creating new principles, establishing new rules for the game, and this is as it should be.

The theatre is a living and dynamic institution and as such is in a constant state of change. Its only alternative is to perish. It was Stark Young who said: "The skillful playwright keeps the theatre alive, but the man of ideas makes it grow." These men of ideas are always in the minority as they seek out new methods or techniques to attain their goals.

It is not the province of this book to cite *all* the many efforts to replace realism, nor is it its province to trace the history of how we arrived at today's theatre fare. Rather it is our purpose to point out what those who create our theatre are *trying* to do. Only then can we apply the three questions of Goethe with some intellectual honesty.

In our opinion, the conventional theatre in this century has been challenged by at least three different forms of avant-garde. Each has brought its own original ideas, but there has also been considerable overlapping. All have been equally well founded and sincere. These three forms are the epic theatre of Bertolt Brecht; the intellectual and philosophical theatre of Luigi Pirandello and Jean-Paul Sartre; and the theatre of cruelty and theatre of the absurd inspired by Antonin Artaud and followed by Eugène Ionesco, Samuel Beckett, Jean Genet, Harold Pinter, and many, many others (with less success).

THE EPIC: BERTOLT BRECHT (1898–1956)

Truth is an absolute.
and should be taught from the stage.

Bertolt Brecht has done more to shape the modern theatre than any playwright since Ibsen. The epic theatre came into being in 1928 with his two memorable plays *The Good Soldier Schweik* and *The Three-Penny Opera*. It is interesting to note that though the word "epic" is associated with his name, it did not originate with him, but with the German, Erwin Piscator, who founded the Epic Proletarian Theatre in 1923.

Brecht began his writing with what he called "learning plays" and throughout his life considered his plays to be lessons or parables rather than imitations of life. He insisted that the stage must always be recognized as a stage and the actors as actors. He wrote this estrangement into his scripts by using prologues and epilogues, omitting suspense, referring to himself as the author and to the play as a play. The audience was invited to judge the actors and the situations rather than to empathize with them, and there was much direct speaking to the audience. All this helped to make the stage really a parable for the world. "What *looked* like a play was really real."

Brecht believed the purpose of the theatre was instructive. Later in his life he would have preferred the name "dialectical" to "epic." He felt that theatre should be used to *teach* the audience how to survive, to serve as a form of demonstration through the use of narrative rather than the performance of an action. He had a fondness for historical subjects and often treated them in very "straight" style. *Galileo* is a biography of a sixteenth-century astronomer and physicist; *Mother Courage* takes place in Poland and Germany during the

70

Thirty Years War. Even his parables of China and those of a wild-and-woolly Chicago that never was, describe real passions and miseries and teem with real people and events. The audience is asked to listen to things that have happened in the past and to reflect on the lessons to be learned from these events of long ago. (This is why the name epic was chosen—it was strictly an historical report of past events.) The dramatic mechanism was to function in the same way as a lecture hall. Instead of the audience feeling, they were to think. Instead of becoming emotionally involved in the performance, they were to adopt an attitude of inquiry and criticism. Brecht's aim was not to provide the audience with an aesthetic experience, but to stimulate them to take a practical stand in matters concerning their own welfare and that of their country. He wished to inhibit their emotional identification with the characters and situations and to avoid tragic catastrophe and substitute for it a vision of a better world. The source was often a parable, with the emphasis on theme rather than on complications of plot or character development. His plays are often "dramas of ideas" through the use of parables. In *The Good Woman of Setzuan* he shows the difficulty of being civilized in an uncivilized world, and in *The Caucasian Chalk Circle*, with its socialist theme, he points out that things should belong to those who know best how to use them. The epic is oftentimes called a drama of themes. There is none of the obscurity of language and situation found in the plays of the so-called absurdist playwrights. Neither would we call Brecht unduly "intellectual" despite the onstage discussions and lectures that he used in preference to dramatic events.

Brecht encouraged detachment—an emotional coolness—so that the audience could take pleasure in understanding what it saw, rather than feeling what it saw. He deplores the audience with heart and nerves and applauded the audience that tempered its feelings with knowledge and observation. In 1936 he stated his attitude:

> The spectator of the dramatic theatre says: "Yes, I have felt the same. I am just like this. This is only natural. It will always be like this. This human being's suffering moves me because there is no way out for him. This is great art; it bears the mark of the inevitable. I am weeping with those who weep on the stage, laughing with those who laugh."
>
> The spectator of the *epic* theatre says: "I should never have thought so. That is not the way to do it. This is most surprising, hardly credible. This will have to stop. This human being's suffering moves me because there would have been a way out for him. This is great art; nothing here seems inevitable. I am laughing about those who weep on the stage, weeping about those who laugh." *

* Kenneth Tynan, *Curtains* (New York: Atheneum Publishers, 1961).

He sought a staging that would meet the needs of a new, revolutionary, scientific age. He turned to old theatrical conventions and traditions: the Greek chorus, the Elizabethan and Oriental theatre, the clown and circus entertainers. He wanted to overcome the theatre of illusion by making the audience ever conscious of being in a theatre—watching a demonstration that had been arranged for the purpose of analysis. Acts were broken into scenes—each with its separate structure. One scene could be a discussion, a narration, a realistic action, a song, or a recitation. The only means of unification was the basic theme. The sequence of scenes could be rearranged, for there was no straining toward a climax or the cumulative effect of the realistic theatre. The scenes were interspersed with projected slogans, slides, signs, pantomime, dance, song, and motion pictures. Bold white light was used instead of atmospheric lighting; half curtains that expose the backstage, well-worn props, a revolving stage, lighting instruments, all were exposed in order to achieve an effect of distance, breaking a spell once it had been established. The development of the plot—though the parable or story is usually given the emphasis—followed curved rather than straight lines. In construction there was no adherence to the well-made-play form.

Brecht has found great success in the professional theatres throughout Europe. Only in the United States has he failed in the commercial theatre, although his influence has been felt in such works as Arthur Kopit's *Indians*, Howard Sackler's *Great White Hope*, and Robert Bolt's *A Man for All Seasons*. All are examples of narrative realism. He has been the idol of the college campuses and educational theatres, and here, too, his influence may be even more important in the future.

Much has been made of Brecht's being non-Aristotelian, and in many respects he was, but not because of his nonuse of empathy. Aristotle said nothing about empathy and estrangement. This was credited to him through later translations. Brecht was not fully pleased with the word "alienation." It comes from *verfremdung*, which can also be translated as "made strange." One wonders if sometime in the future the whole of this theory might not be more aptly called "Brechtian theatre."

The most common criticisms of his work are that he preaches rather than dramatizes his ideas—that he reduces the theatre to political partisanship, often makes symbols of his characters instead of real people, and mechanizes the theatre.

The following chart contrasts the substance, form, and technique of the dramatic and epic goals. The whole of the avant-garde movement has borrowed liberally from Brecht's conception of the theatre.

The Epic Theatre of Bertolt Brecht

Brecht eliminates from his theatre: illusion—unity—emotional involvement—identification—empathy—catharsis.

He uses: choral passages—lyrics—narrations—symbols—motion pictures—slides—visual aids—anything to imitate real life, so long as it *is obviously* a means of projecting his imitation.

The Epic Theatre	The Dramatic Theatre
Creates events that have little need for sequence, moves in "irregular" curves.	Creates sequence of events that move in a straight line.
Makes the spectator an observer to action, arouses activity.	Involves the spectator empathically.
Strives for alienation—a feeling apart, to make us investigate the character intellectually.	Strives for audience identification with characters.
Awakes man's energy to make him act and to make decisions.	Uses man's energy vicariously.
Demands discussion, uses arguments.	Allows for feelings.
Only gives bits of knowledge—we must fill in.	Communicates the experiences of the characters.
Makes us strictly "observers" of the action.	Involves us "in" the action.
Is filled with arguments to arouse our thinking.	Is filled with suggestion to feed our imagination.
Presents man as an object of investigation who can change.	Presents man as a known quantity who is not easily changed.
Interests us in what is happening *now* in the action.	Interests us in the conclusion of the story.
Pictures the world as what it is becoming.	Presents the world as it is in the playwright's vision.
Presents a series of disconnected events with as little plot as possible.	Emphasizes the plot.

Points up all the theatrical aids to make us aware of the theatre and the mechanical aspects of theatricality.	Masks theatre aids such as lights, scenery, sound effects, etc.
Believes in theatre as an instrument of social change: a lecture-hall, pulpit, school to stimulate thought, so that instead of sharing a problem the audience must come to grips with it.	Believes in theatre as a means for escape, entertainment, enlightenment, literature, beauty; a pause in life, a recognition of problems and crises in the lives of imagined characters.

ANTI-THEATRE AND THE RELATIVITY OF TRUTH:
LUIGI PIRANDELLO (1867–1936)

The theatre and reality cannot meet
without destroying each other.

This giant of the unorthodox came into prominence in 1921 with his highly theatrical masterpiece *Six Characters in Search of an Author*. Released from both logic and verisimilitude, Pirandello developed great surrealistic qualities. He had revived theatricality, which realism and naturalism had almost destroyed. When Bernard Shaw saw this play in performance he is reported to have said: "This playwright is greater than I am."

A group of actors are in rehearsal for a rather inconsequential play. They are interrupted by six characters who have been created by a playwright and never used. They demand the stage to enact their story. The "real" actors try to impersonate the "unreal" characters, but the intruders are more alive than the real actors. Both common sense and scientific views of reality are attacked. We begin to question what is real and what is unreal. Pirandello has shattered the surface appearance of life without abandoning it. Symbolism and expressionism had taken over.

In this script the playwright broke ground for what we have come to call "anti-theatre." All the usual elements of the dramatist were abandoned. There was no plot. The characters were enmeshed in reality and illusion—the real or the unreal—as actor or as character. It was almost impossible to find a theme, at least one that could be stated in a few words. Audiences were moved, excited, enthralled, intrigued. Many returned to see the play time and time again as the whole question of reality and truth took on new meanings.

Pirandello's work embodies a search, an exploration of consciousness. He felt that a major portion of our mental and emotional life goes unseen. We lead life dually, in the conscious and the subconscious.

Man is no longer a creature with a rational soul or an individual self, but a creature with *many* selves who is far less rational than he appears on the surface. Reason is a delusion. Reality is confused and confusing—always changing. Ethics are relative. Life's greatest absurdity is trying to find out what is the "truth," for all truth is relative. Appearances are faulty, and lying is a necessity.

Every man must wear a mask to protect himself from the gossips of the world. That mask is always changing as he develops and as different people see him through different eyes and circumstances. Let us imagine that the most candid descriptions of a man's character (without the use of names, dates, or locales) have been written by a number of individuals, including: a blood relative (mother, father, sister, or brother), an employer who has dismissed him for unsatisfactory work, the teacher of his favorite subjects, in which he had been the outstanding student, his wife, a second teacher who had been forced to fail him for his lack of progress and poor attitude, a minister who had failed to interest him in attending church services, his closest personal friend over many years, a banker with whom there has just been a very successful or unsuccessful transaction, the personnel man at his favorite club, and himself. In studying all these descriptions could we imagine they were of one man? The answer is an emphatic "no," for one can never penetrate another's identity; beneath the assumed self lies another indistinct self. Each man discovers reality for himself and is incapable of translating it for others. A realistic style would pigeonhole this character with a single adjective.

Pirandello's revolt from the naturalistic conventions involved a greater use of the imagination by both playwright and audience. His world was the world of the intellect, but it was not undramatic.

He could never see why man gave so much attention to a tangible reality when that reality was in a constant state of flux, offering nothing that was solid or permanent. The only real aspects of a brief life were our memories of what had been and our dreams of what yet might be. He delved deeply into the secret chambers of man's heart and discovered their tragic wants—their isolation, and he found that words were a most inadequate means of expression.

His characters rebel at instinct. Man is compelled to yield to it even when perfectly aware of its dire consequences. His characters resent having their whole lives identified with a moment of weakness. His dreams begin where instinct ends. His characters are people who give themselves to passion, but cannot live in it. His pessimism has humor and laughter—a laughter that hurts, even as it relieves the tension.

Pirandello's fixation with his relativity of sanity and truth, drama and reality, made him a leader in the anti-drama of despair in the 1920s.

He did not inspire hope, but he did illuminate the destiny of man in his time. As psychology and physical science accepted the relativity of knowledge, the world came to accept the substance in his theatre of implication. He had never appealed greatly to the masses, and by the 1930s he, as an avant-garde playwright, had become fixed in history and readily accepted by the more conventional theatre. The new playwrights of the 1950s, in their attempt to portray the varying levels of consciousness, were quick to adopt his techniques, and we must cite his influence on the drama of the existentialists and the absurd. His linear descendants are Beckett and Ionesco, along with Albee, Cocteau, Anouilh, and Pinter, who are all greatly in his debt.

EXISTENTIALISM: JEAN-PAUL SARTRE (B. 1905)

Every man must find out his own way.

Jean-Paul Sartre is an existentialist philosopher turned playwright who has used the theatre for the presentation of his philosophical leanings. His playwriting career began in 1943 and 1944 with *The Flies* and *No Exit*, both of which projected the existential philosophy that says every man must make a choice and be wholly responsible for whatever may result from that choice.

Webster defines existentialism as "a literary-philosophic cult of nihilism and pessimism, popularized in France after World War II, chiefly by Jean-Paul Sartre: it holds that each man exists as an individual in a purposeless universe, and that he must oppose his hostile environment through the exercise of his free will." "Nihilism" is the denial of the existence of any basis for knowledge or truth—the general rejection of customary beliefs in morality, religion, etc. Both of these dictionary definitions are too extreme, though—as in most movements—some of Sartre's followers have gone much further than he in their implementation, especially in their nihilism.

In 1946 Sartre expressed the essentials of his goals in an article entitled: "Forgers of Myths." In it he pointed out that existentialist playwrights were not concerned with psychology, which they considered the most abstract of the sciences, where a single word might "explain" an act or a passion. They demanded a new drama divorced from the realistic theatre, where stories were told of "defeat, laissez-faire, and drifting—preferring to show how external forces batter a man to pieces, destroy him bit by bit. The existentialist seeks the true realism, for he knows it is impossible in everyday life to distinguish between fact and right, real and ideal, psychology and ethics."

Sartre was not interested in portraying individual personalities or universal types, but rather desired to "speak in terms of [the masses] most general preoccupations, dispelling their anxieties in the form of myths that anyone can understand and feel deeply—such as the great myths of death, exile, love." In forming these myths he did not want the play, the characters, or the situations to seem familiar. For this purpose he enhanced or enlarged the images to increase the distance and minimize the relationship between the play and the audience. Thus, the audience could *see* its own sufferings rather than experience them. The play was to be concerned with only one event—a conflict about rights in a general situation—short, terse in style, with a small cast and the characters thrown into a contest where they are forced to make a choice.

Eric Bentley classified Sartre as part of the absurd movement and called his plays "philosophic melodramas," for they do contain torture, lynchings, suicide, executions, rape, murder, bombings, and civil and uncivil war, but Martin Esslin, the real authority on the theatre of the absurd, does not feel that Sartre's works belong there. It is true that the basis of existentialist thought emphasizes that being in the world is absurd and that man must be aware of that absurdity, but existentialism allows him to carve his own destiny and contends that man is determined by his acts. Here it departs from the true absurd philosophy—where there is no choice. Further, Esslin points out that the absurdists employ more discontinuity and fragmentation and put much less emphasis on plot and characterization; that their interest lies more in the audience asking "What is happening?" than "How will it end?"

Sartre does use cruelty in dialogue to attain the metaphysical exploration that Artaud would have approved, but he is too logical. In *No Exit* the characters try to understand their damnation and thus explain Sartre's definition of both death and hell, where identity is fixed forever and choice no longer exists. In *The Flies* Orestes rebels against the universe of Jupiter and tries to force his people to rebel also. He not only frees them, he challenges them to engage their freedom in a cause. These acts are too positive for the absurdists.

The world of Sartre is preoccupied with three aspects of man's existence: (1) his alienation and aloneness; (2) his freedom; and (3) his responsibility. Each man lives in his own world and can never really communicate with other worlds, but his conscience is his freedom, and this freedom allows man to make a choice. By making that choice man exists and thus creates himself, but man is constantly trying to avoid that choosing. He makes alibis daily and curses the routines of life. It is the fear of loneliness and of the unknown that forces him to follow these routines. At the same time his aloneness is contradicted by his desire to assume responsibility as a human being and to join some cause. Thus tension grows within man to such proportions that there is a great anguish and a feeling of life's absurdity. The decision once made brings about the responsibility of having to face and live with the consequences of that decision—of having created himself. In this sense existentialism is a positive philosophy, for man *can* decide. Those who out of fear do not act are committing a worse crime in not making this effort for freedom. Man must make his difficult way through a world that God has deserted and in which economic and psychological determinism can no longer be used as excuses. The philosophy is close to Nietzsche's "God does not exist," for since man creates his own existence there is no need for a supernatural being. The philosophy fitted well into the thinking of post-occupation France, when she was once again trying to find herself.

In *Existentialism is a Humanism*, Sartre wrote:

> What the existentialist says is that the coward develops into a coward, the hero develops into a hero; there is always a possibility that the coward will be one no longer, that the hero will be one no longer. What counts is the total commitment, and you are not totally committed by a particular circumstance, a particular action.

Sartre is deeply concerned about a code of ethics for modern man in a world deprived of supernatural sanctions. He poses the problem of heroism in each individual action, for man in making his ethical choice does—in a sense—choose for all men.

Sartre is more concerned with content than with structure and follows rather closely the well-made play formula. His plays are more romantic than realistic and are not considered as great today as they were thought to be in the forties. If Sartre is not a member of the absurd group, he did open the door that made the absurdists possible. We can, therefore, consider him a forerunner of Samuel Beckett, Eugène Ionesco, Edward Albee, and even Harold Pinter, whose dramas of the absurd, of hostility, disgust, and nothingness, were to find audiences later on. What he had to say had validity.

Few would have imagined in the mid-forties that only twenty years later we in the United States would be experiencing much of the nihilism expressed in his philosophy and that to a greater or lesser degree our whole society would be in what may justly be called an existentialist period.

THE ABSURDISTS

The chaos after World War I and World War II gave us:

Brecht (1928), with his theory of estrangement, destruction of illusion and reinforcement of aesthetic distance, and return to theatricalism.

Pirandello (1921), with his preoccupation with the nature of truth, philosophy of pessimism supported by humor, and anti-theatre approach that reduced the importance of both story and character.

Sartre (1943–1944), with his existentialism, emphasis on nihilism, and use of myths for substance and of the word *absurd* to describe life.

In the early fifties, the times were propitious for the strongest attack of all by the avant-garde. The conventional and realistic theatre was suffering more than ever from the lack of new ideas, new playwrights, and new blood.

The whole world, still in the shadow of World War II, was in a state of revolution. Our reverence for logic, reason, and science had enabled us to develop instant world-wide communication, the hydrogen bomb, air conditioning, computerized production, and the possibility of space travel, but we still knew little about ourselves and the reason for our being on earth. Our logic had produced only the illogical. We were still faced with poverty, race hatred, the inability to build mental hospitals fast enough to meet the demand, juvenile delinquency, dope addiction, murder in the streets, and wars that had, in the twentieth century, killed ninety-six million men, women, and children while devastating whole countries. All this we saw vividly. Finally, we had to admit that there was some meaninglessness and absurdity in our very existence.

This absurdity was first expressed in the theatre by Eugène Ionesco in *The Bald Soprano* in 1950 and then by Samuel Beckett's *Waiting for Godot* in 1953, but to understand the absurd we must go back to its very roots.

Just as Strindberg had planted the seed of expressionism at the end of the last century, so had an obscure personality, Alfred Jarry (1873–1907), whom we have already introduced on page 2, sown the seed of absurdity. Jarry felt that "recounting comprehensible things only serves to make heavy the spirit and to warp the memory, whereas the absurd exercises the spirit and makes memory work." His writings (none worthy of mention here) reflected the same chaos and illogical quality of his personal life where he found "alcohol his 'holy water' " and the "very essence of life." His direct influence was short-lived but was reflected to some extent in Dadaism in 1916–1922. This strange artistic style—fantastic, symbolic, often formlessly expressionistic of subconscious matter—never really caught on in the theatre, but it showed its influence in Apollinaire's play *The Breasts of Tiresias,* in 1917. There are some authorities who credit Apollinaire with having created the word "surrealism" in its preface. The author defined it as "returning to nature without imitating her photographically." The dictionary definition is: "A modern movement in art and literature, in which an attempt is made to portray or interpret the workings of the subconscious mind as manifested in dreams: it is characterized by an irrational, non-contextual arrangement of material."

The Theatre of Cruelty: Antonin Artaud (1896–1948)

It remained, however, for another man, Antonin Artaud, to develop the whole concept with a work called *The Theatre and Its Double* (its double being life), which was published in 1938 and immediately became the bible of the avant-garde.

The book is difficult to grasp in its entirety and even more difficult to summarize, for Artaud was a visionary and a mystic. It was published while the author was a patient in a hospital for the insane, where he spent nine of the last ten years of his life. Artaud may easily be considered the mad genius of the century.

In the beginning he was a confirmed surrealist, being greatly affected by the metaphysical theatre of the Orient—especially the Balinese theatre. To him the Occidental theatre of psychology was extremely childish and gross. He felt that:

> The theatre should set up vibrations not on a single level, but on every level of the mind at once. . . . pure theatre will be an elucidation of the most abstract themes—inventing a language of gestures to be developed in space—a language without meaning except in the circumstances of the stage—and in addition to an acute sense of plastic beauty, these gestures have as their final goal the elucidation of a spiritual state or problem.

In 1927 he broke with the theories of surrealism in order to write and stage his own surrealistic plays. This was partially due to political differences but largely in the hope of making money. He aimed at a theatre of magic, myth, astonishment, and cruelty. In 1935 he founded his short-lived Theatre of Cruelty and staged his own play, *The Cenci*, adapted from Shelley with the aid of Stendahl. Even with the help of Jean-Louis Barrault it was a financial and artistic fiasco and a primary cause of his mental breakdown.

The theatre of cruelty should not be associated with violence and the sensational. "Cruelty," for Artaud, meant "shock," and his conception called for the use of genuine ritual and magic mingled with the excitement of stylized movement: lavish staging, a de-emphasis of language, and playing up of the irrational. He wanted the spectators to be involved to the point that the inner organs of the body were affected rather than the mind—a kind of steam bath of the senses—

leaving the audience shocked and tingling in every emotional pore. The substance of the theatre of cruelty was ritual, based on myth, symbol, sorcery, and gesture, together with speech and visual actions that so shocked the audience that it became a part of the dramatic action. His actors would actually assault the spectators by mingling with them, drawing them physically into the action. He once said: "Without an element of cruelty at the root of every spectacle the theatre is not possible. In our present state of degeneration it is through the skin that metaphysics must be made to reenter our minds."

Artaud felt that the theatre should not attempt to analyze character or be concerned with the individual but should identify itself with the masses, and for this reason the spoken language was unnecessary. The source of his substance was ideas of a cosmic nature that touched on such issues as creation, being, and chaos, which by their very nature could not be formally illustrated by language.

Artaud's greatest weakness lay in his failure to see more than his own point of view. He lacked any sense of moderation. Once he had discovered the value of metaphysics, magic, and the excitement that was available through the use of various stage and production effects— which he called *mise-en-scène* ("putting on the stage")—he forsook all of the values that were present in the nineteenth- and twentieth-century psychological and realistic theatre. What he failed to see was that the "putting on the stage" was far more in the province of the director and the production than in that of playwright and script.

Nevertheless, Artaud and Brecht must be considered this century's greatest innovators in the theatre. Brecht's scripts never quite fitted into his epic theory as successfully as did the acting and the production areas, but he did furnish us with scripts. Artaud's theories were far more influential than were any of his scripts, though he went to his grave in 1948 convinced that his life and his influence on the theatre had been for naught.

The Theatre of the Absurd

These two men, with their theories, helped to create a new theatre— the anti-theatre of our times. Their followers, who became the leaders of this anti-theatre, quickly adapted to their own use all that Brecht, Pirandello, Sartre, and Artaud had given them, and with the addition of their own principles and techniques the theatre of the absurd came into existence. It was a theatre so different that analysis was at first difficult. Many called it a theatre devoid of meaning, a theatre without a purpose or a goal, for often it did not even possess a logical sentence structure.

The audience, accustomed to a rigidly constructed story with characters they knew in situations they could recognize in a play with a beginning, a middle, and an end, found it highly difficult to adjust to what they saw and heard. All was so bizarre, so strange, so disconnected that they could only cry out: "I did not understand anything I saw!" The absurdists' only answer was that understanding—in the traditional sense—was not even intended; that the goal was for the audience to relax, settle back, watch what it saw, enjoy what it could, and recognize the very existence of absurdity, for in a *world* without meaning, why should there be a meaningful *theatre?*

On the other hand, there were those who argued that the whole anti-theatre movement was *not* antagonistic to meaning—that it was highly intellectual and did demand study, careful analysis, interpretation, and after-thought; that there was a far greater intellectual depth than could be found in the conventional theatre. They compared it to the work of the Surrealists, the Dadaists, the Impressionists in painting who saw life through the imagination rather than through the lens of a camera.

These advocates of the absurd have pointed out that Brecht's alienation is always present, for here the world is pictured as incomprehensible. The audience observes the action without ever grasping the full meaning of what it sees. Without this comprehension it cannot relate to the characters on stage, and thus cannot share their emotions. The audience senses that the action does have some vague relationship to life, but that it is absurd and pointless. Intellectually, the spectator recognizes in the style the irrationality he has sensed subconsciously in his own existence. He begins to associate the grotesque antics on the stage with his contemporary world.

Where the conventional theatre worked with a specific framework and attempted to picture life as photographically as possible by pointing up a definite problem and recognizing characters with a will moving toward its solution, the absurd has no special goal. There is no beginning and no end. It is all middle—one unknown moves to another unknown. While the traditional theatre is plot-centered, the epic theatre is theme-centered, and the absurd theatre is tone- or mood-centered.

Suspense is supplied in the conventional theatre by the spectator's wondering what will happen next—how the story will end. In the absurd the suspense—which every theatre must have—grows out of the audience's wondering what unpredictable thing might occur next and how it might possibly relate to something that will help them to understand *what* is going on. Esslin insists that:

In this sense, the Theatre of the Absurd is the most demanding, the most intellectual theatre. It may be riotously funny, wildly exaggerated and over-simplified, vulgar and garish, but will always confront the spectator with a genuine intellectual problem, a philosophical paradox, which he will have to try to solve even if he knows that it is most probably insoluble.

The three playwrights most prominent in the theatre of the absurd are Beckett, Ionesco, and Genet. It is as if these three look upon Ibsen and Shaw as teachers who ineffectively shook their fingers at man and scolded him about his sociological, moral, and religious problems. They look beyond such personal details, and when they do they see only a hopeless mass of ignorance, a life that is not only unjust but absurd. Their theatre or schoolroom is metaphysical rather than sociological.

We shall now turn to these three dramatists and briefly consider the substance and techniques of each. A fourth name, that of Harold Pinter, the English playwright, has been added. He borrows much from the absurd, but is more a combination of absurd and conventional theatre. He is considered the most promising current playwright.

The Absurdity of Language: Eugene Ionesco (b. 1912)

Ionesco, like many intellectuals, looked down on the theatre and once said: "I started writing for the theatre because I hated it." The major portion of his work falls into the "anti-theatre" category. He has accordingly become one of the most popular of the avant-garde playwrights.

While studying English with a "French-English Conversation Manual," he conceived the idea of writing a skit satirizing the foolish conversations found in the exercises. Out of it grew what we know as The Bald Soprano. He would read it aloud to friends and at parties "just for laughs." An enterprising director saw its possibilities and got his permission to present it as a one-act play. Ionesco was embarked as the first in a new school that would come to be called the theatre of the absurd.

It will be remembered that Sartre first used the word absurd to describe man's existence in his discussions of existentialism. The topic became popular because of an "essay on the absurd" by a follower of Sartre, Albert Camus. Published in 1942, The Myth of Sisyphus proposed "a description in pure form of an illness of the spirit." The essay proclaimed a permanent gap that existed between self and surroundings. Camus found reality and experiences were irremediably separate.

Through all his work Ionesco was to emphasize that words had no real meaning and that conversation was hopeless as a means of communication. His contention was that words only obscured the truth that might lie beyond or underneath; that one word only called to mind another of a similar sound. Facts, perhaps, could be known, but truth was an experience. He said: "The dream is pure drama. In a dream one is always in mid-situation . . . I think that the dream is a lucid thought, more lucid than any that one has when awake, a thought expressed in images, and that at the same time its form is always dramatic." At his best he has been true to his dreams. He has put his nightmares on the stage with an uncanny sense of what works there. The submerged fantasies of violence and terror in middle-class life come through.

With the possible exception of the old couple in *The Chairs* and surely Berringer in *The Killer, Rhinoceros,* and *Exit the King,* the characters in Ionesco's plays lack any real depth or substance. They are sudden and two-dimensional like the figures in a dream—simple and machine-made. They are always surrounded by things, overpowered by matter, which is of little importance and only serves to crowd them out of their worlds. Whatever his desires, he is a dramatist of images rather than ideas.

Ionesco demands that the theatre be pure theatre; that it abandon all the principles that have been established by the conventional drama. He promotes exaggeration of all kinds—in character—in story—in acting. All life should be amplified beyond reality. This is at the heart of much of his humor and does create considerable laughter in production. His plays are, for this reason, often considered comedies. Tragi-farce would be a better term, for—submerged—there is always a real sadness, a sense of tragedy as the thinking audience recognizes the absurdity in life that is represented by his images.

He always insists that he is opposed to presenting philosophies or themes in his plays and for this reason rejects Sartre and his existentialism (with the exception of *No Exit*) and, especially, Brecht with his Marxist leanings. Nevertheless, Ionesco is always interested in discovering some means of eliminating the confusion and futility of life that he emphasizes.

Few dramatists have written so prolifically in defense of their own works. His plays have been both lucid and meaningful, but his rationalizations are far less illuminating than the works themselves.

The Absurdity of Life: Samuel Becket (b. 1906)

> Nothing happens, nobody comes, nobody goes,
> it's awful.
>
> —*From* Waiting for Godot

Samuel Beckett was awarded the Nobel Prize in Literature in 1969. This honor was also awarded to Pirandello in 1934 and to Sartre in 1964, although Sartre chose to decline it. Beckett's greatest play is

Waiting for Godot, which many consider to be the best, if not the only play of the absurd that will live. In all his works Beckett shows his existential background with its emptiness, pessimism, frustrations, despair, and constant grappling with death. He, even more than Ionesco, finds man lost in a world deserted by God and reason, where the individual is eternally trapped. Beckett's key is absence, loneliness, nothingness, while man waits for the only certainty—death—which is the greatest absurdity of all.

There is virtually no intrigue or action in his plays. What there is, goes in a circular fashion. There is much facial expression, many useless gestures that have no meaning at all. Man puts on and takes off his hat or shoes and putters around, picking up and putting down, looking out the window and seeing nothing, suggesting in a kind of non-verbal language the anguish and ennui of everyday existence. It all adds up to impressionistic theatre, in which the audience feels as bored and alienated and alone as do the characters on the stage. This tone or mood is a substitute for the suspense one usually demands of the theatre.

The theme comes back again and again: Man needs affection and fellowship. This is the only thing that makes life bearable. The theme is emphasized by his use of characters in pairs: Pozo and Lucky, Didi and Go Go in *Waiting for Godot*; Clove and Ham, Nell and Nagg in *Endgame*; and Krapp and his tape in *Krapp's Last Tape*. These couples may disagree, quarrel, get on each other's nerves, but they do have and need each other.

The characters themselves are little more than symbols. There is little or no psychological development, and the language they speak is absurd—the same story told over and over, the same questions asked —constant repetitions. They are alive and believable because they do represent humanity in general. It is difficult to relate to them, but even while the spectator laughs, it is with sympathy for their condition. He can sense their existential anguish. It is a kind of substitution for the pity and fear of Aristotle, just as one laughs when one sees others make fools of themselves or experience some physical mishap. But the laughter of Beckett is a kind of cosmic laughter. It is a laugh that François Villon was referring to when he wrote: "I laugh, in order that I may not cry."

Involvement in Beckett is of an inner or visceral nature as well as intellectual. His plays, for this reason, need to be seen rather than read, for they are made up of symbols and symbolic overtones. One has to give himself over to them to appreciate what lies beyond the lines and action.

When Beckett was asked by a director what he meant in *Waiting for Godot,* his answer was: "If I'd have known, I would have put it in the play." This could be said of all his plays, for, when witnessing one, the spectator must fit himself into the play and find his own myth—

get out of it what he can. Beckett reduces all the artificiality of culture, civilization, and life itself to absurdity. Each man takes it unto himself to find the meaning that Beckett put there.

The Ritual in Theatre: Jean Genet (b. 1907)

Good is only an illusion.
Evil is a Nothingness which arises upon the ruins of Good.

Genet does not really belong to the theatre of the absurd. Beckett and Ionesco have pictured man's tragedy and loneliness in the world but have edged it with comedy. Genet is the extreme of the anti-realistic theatre. He glories in the triumph of evil; he has been a criminal in one way or another since childhood. He has been intimately associated with thievery, perversion, drugs, and smuggling since at the age of ten he was arrested for stealing and decided then to become what society wished to make him. This he has accomplished with a vengeance. For much of his life he has served prison terms throughout Europe. Sartre, whose philosophy Genet has lived, has called him the greatest artist of our times and has written the story of his life in *Saint Genet, Actor and Martyr*, in which he pictures Genet as rejected by the world and therefore turning to the evil.

As a playwright, Genet exerts this same genuine act of aggression. He depicts his world of alienation and fills his plays with its people. Borrowing from Pirandello the themes of the relativity of truth and role-playing, he allows mirrors to play an important part in most of his plays. Reflections vie with reality until we are no longer sure what is real and what is reflection. Even Genet does not always seem sure which is which and has said: "My characters are all masks."

His plays do have plots and in this sense seem to follow the traditional story lines. Their messages are specific and usually concern social, sexual, or political problems. However, his viewpoint is ultimately contrary to the accepted one. He defends his own personal view of life and rationalizes all his anti-social behavior. He finds beauty in perversion, evil, and the ugly. There is far more of Jarry in Genet's surrealism than in either Beckett's or Ionesco's. In fact, these three playwrights have nothing in common beyond their general surrealistic style.

Genet's greatest strength is evident when he gives way to purely emotional and artistic drives. Then he gives us raw dramatic experience, always at its best in ritualistic ceremonies that exaggerate sex and crime in his bizzare stories.

His finest play is *The Balcony*. The scene is the interior of a house of prostitution, where three men have come to experience their own illusions. One is dressed as a bishop, one as a general, and one a judge, roles they could not play in life. Here they view themselves in the mirror and live their dreams. There is a revolution in the country, and the queen is killed. The madame of the brothel is given the chance to play the role of the queen, and the three men do become what they have always dreamed of being—bishop, general, and judge. Once this realization is achieved, they find they can no longer dream. Reality is neither as great nor as satisfying as the lie.

In his preface to *The Maids* Genet condemned the triviality of the conventional theatre and called for one of communion, ceremony, and awe. Thus, ritual is the heart of his plays. There is always a kind of religious worship, but in reverse order. Evil is in the ascendancy, replacing good. The devil becomes God, and a love of perverted beauty replaces religious faith. His characters are all criminals, outcasts, prostitutes, and reprobates, who have been ostracized by the world's more virtuous people. These characters are all reflections of Genet's own life. In the theatre in proper hands Genet can be effective. The intensity of his spell lasts for the duration of a performance. On reflection it loses that power, for it is all so foreign to any experience the spectator has known. His theatricality and his bizarre approach to life, backed by the ritual of a "religious" experience, mislead the audience. No writer today more completely represents the truly theatrical.

Appearance versus Reality: Harold Pinter (b. 1930)

Harold Pinter has denied that he belongs to the absurdist group. Certainly he has discovered a mid-point between the full-fledged absurdist and the realistic theatre, for he has managed to combine the basic conventional theatre's mystery, suspense, and comedy with the sense of strangeness and unreality of the avant-garde.

He does admit that his work has been influenced by Samuel Beckett, and he is an existentialist who believes that human nature is neither fixed nor ordained by laws or edicts. He sees man as defining himself from moment to moment by his acts. These acts are often contradictory, which permits them to be completely unexpected and thus furnish great theatrical values. As with Beckett, much of what he means to say is left unsaid, and both men make the "pause" almost part of the dialogue.

Pinter also denies that his plays possess a symbolic content, but to read one—and certainly to see one—is to realize that they do possess vast metaphysical overtones. One leaves a Pinter play feeling that one knows what it was about, for there *is* a superficial meaning or story line, even though the plot is never strongly developed. Once out of the theatre, moreover, we do not forget the play. It comes back to mind, and we realize there are other levels of meaning and that much more was said than we had thought. There is always some new shading that strikes the imagination and makes us look for more beneath the surface.

He gives us pleasure on both the literal and reflective levels. Someone has called Pinter "outwardly lucid and inwardly impenetrable."

He is a master at being almost completely incommunicative while talking. His characters are kept at a great distance through their use of words. They are behind a smoke screen, speaking in words we know—but we do not always know what the words mean when they are spoken. He is most aware of the language that lies beneath language, and makes the unsaid word sometimes louder than the spoken.

Pinter has said: "I'd say that what goes on in my plays is realistic, but what I'm doing is not realistic." This is an apt description, for while his work approaches the well-made play formula, he does leave many questions unanswered; his exposition is very meager—especially as to what has occurred before the opening of the play; and his characters and their motivations are only vaguely suggested. It is in this manner that he tantalizes the audience. He seems to have struck a perfect combination of obscurity and the obvious.

The setting of Pinter's plays is usually a livingroom, realistically furnished. It is, though, a macabre kind of realism. The characters are natural enough. They speak a dialogue that is easy-going with its foolish repetitions and clichés, but suddenly there creeps in through the conversation an ominous note. We begin to feel that just outside there are dangers—that something dreadful is going to happen. He has a great talent for producing this sense of mystery and suspense, as he reinforces the feeling of man being lost and the terror of insecurity in a complacent world. There is just enough humor to accent this feeling of melodrama so that it becomes both humorous and frightening. John Gassner has called it "comically melodramatic and melodramatically comic"—constituting a wholly new dramatic type.

Pinter's style is unique, for while his plays seem real, he is always a step away from reality—presenting the impossible in the guise of the actual. He has a keen sense of the theatre and manages to integrate his humor while he tricks, beguiles, confuses, and alarms his audience. He is difficult to pin down specifically, for as The New Yorker said in its review of The Caretaker: "He is mysterious, frightening, funny, and altogether remarkable."

It is little wonder that Pinter is considered the most original playwright of the English language in our modern theatre. Critics have already coined the word "Pinteresque," which he dislikes, but which is a great tribute to a dramatist barely past forty years of age.

SUMMARY

We want to make it clear that the four playwrights we have chosen for discussion are, in our opinion, the leaders of the avant-garde movement. There are many others whose work has been, to a greater or lesser degree, a part of this trend. The list below is both limited and arbitrary, but each has made his personal contribution.

In France, Albert Camus and Arthur Adamov were prominent, though the latter did return to the more conventional theatre. Jean Giraudoux and Jean Anouilh both veered from the conventional but still held great popularity in the strictly commercial theatre. In Germany and Switzerland, Peter Weiss, Friedrich Durrenmatt, and Rolf Hochhuth are notable. In England, John Osborne was the first to be recognized as an "angry young man" but he, too, turned back toward center soon after his initial success. Robert Bolt, Arnold Wesker, Peter Shaffer, and, most recently, Tom Stoppard have made worthy contributions to the London stage. Edward Albee was the leader in the United States. He made great strides, but he has also become more and more conventional in his work. Jack Gelber, Megan Terry, Arthur Kopit, and Jean-Claude van Itallie are worthy of mention.

There have been, as always, many far smaller talents who saw in the absurd a theatre that, although apparently without form or sense, was both profitable and easy and who clambered aboard. In a period noted for its dearth of playwrights, many of these managed to be seen. Most had used shock for the sake of shock, or novelty for the sake of novelty, rather than for credibility or enlightenment. The result only helped to give the whole movement an unfortunate reputation. *Time* magazine, in 1966, characterized their efforts as a serious dialogue that was: ". . . difficult, oblique and garbled. It sometimes seems like a bad phone connection—full of static, elusive, abrupt, frustrating, and almost hostile. United States playwrights have even cut the wire—for the moment they have nothing to say about either humanity or the human predicament."

It has become increasingly important for the audience to study each script very carefully for its imagination, its originality, its truth, and its sincerity.

A new avant-garde is needed every few years in spite of the disruptions and destruction it brings to what many consider to be very satisfactory theatre. Each new movement during this century has had the same goal: to improve or eliminate the psychological, realistic theatre that was ever growing more senile.

In the theatre, any avant-garde has but a short life. Either it dies in its efforts to *become* the new theatre, or it serves as a transfusion to the old and ceases to exist as a separate entity. Only in this sense is it important, for it has succeeded in eliminating the no longer useful parts of the older theatre by supplying new modes. Brecht and Pirandello supplied the most successful transfusions in the 1920–1940 period, and thus gave the theatre new life.

The current avant-garde had its roots in the dreams of Jarry and Artaud. Its finest flowering has been the work of Ionesco, Beckett, and Genet. To complete our metaphor, we cast Sartre as mid-wife. Together they belong to the period beginning about mid-century and represent one part of a theatre divided.

On the right we have most of Broadway, the majority of our community theatres, and, on the extreme right, such groups as the American Shakespeare Festival in Stratford, Connecticut. On the left we find, among others, the Judson Poet's Theatre off-off-Broadway, which is given to scripts by obscure playwrights, wild camp musicals, and off-beat original dramas; Ellen Stewart's La Mama Experimental Theatre Club, where a place is made available to avant-garde playwrights to stage their dramas while work on them is still in progress—the only requirement being that they be far left. The most widely known, furthest left, and most controversial is the Living Theatre, headed by Julian Beck and Judith Malina. This group began in a conventional enough manner at the Cherry Lane Theatre off-Broadway in the early fifties. Later it attained its own theatre on 14th Street and began to veer more to the left with its greatest commercial success, Jack Gelber's *The Connection*, dealing with narcotics addictions, and Kenneth H. Brown's *The Brig*, concerning life in a Marine Corps prison, produced with a combination of photographic reality, choreography, and music rhythms. These earlier days showed promise of a brilliant future for an unusually talented company of dedicated actors in search of new theatre forms.

In 1963, the Bureau of Internal Revenue charged the company with non-payment of admission taxes and locked the theatre. Malina and Beck were later sentenced to short prison terms and soon afterward left with the company for Europe, where they became gypsies roaming the countryside and presenting far-left scripts in the Artaud manner, expressing their disenchantment with the *status quo*. In 1968 they returned to the United States, where they have played in New York and on tour as a purely propagandist group, in almost constant conflict with local authorities and the law. Unfortunately, they have chosen to *use* the theatre as a means of projecting their own disillusionment with present conditions and to propagandize their own political and social beliefs.

Even in their translations or adaptations of plays by recognized playwrights the living theatre does more adapting than translating. In their production of Brecht's *Antigone of Sophocles* they spent almost thirty minutes in an actor-audience confrontation before a word was spoken. With much pantomime and wailing the actors spoke muted lines, re-arranged for the purpose of incantation. Save for Antigone and Creon, who were dressed in black, the remainder of the cast appeared in ordinary working clothes. Even the hopeful ending suggested by Brecht is sacrificed for their own emphasis on oppression.

More often than not they leave their audience in a great quandary because of their disdain for any accepted form in playwriting. Instead they choose a haphazard invention that they call a "theatre of chance." The result is chiefly sensual, highly symbolic, strong on rhythms and incantation, and seemingly having as its goal to shock or antagonize.

A less controversial but still propagandist theatre is found in numerous small groups that travel about a city from one area to another—setting up improvised stages in parks, open areas, street corners, supermarkets, and anywhere they might attract an audience. The performances of such groups are called "street theatre." Scripts are usually original or revivals of short skits that have been adapted to current problems. Actors are often dedicated and sincere in their desire for social change through the dramatization of today's issues. Audiences of all ages are frequently seeing their first live drama, and the reaction is much as it might have been in medieval times. Technical effects are at a minimum, acting is broad, and scripts simple but exciting. All is quite unstructured; audience participation is encouraged; the scripts invite improvisation and creation of the moment. Exciting and vital as it may be, however, street theatre barely comes within the bounds of our discussions here.

In the final sentence of our introduction in chapter 1 the hope was expressed that we might live to see the current dichotomy resolved. Today, Pinter may represent the dawn of that new theatre. In some respects he has helped to bridge the chasm between the avant-garde on the left and the conventional on the right. Only time will tell.

At the risk of overgeneralizing, we have summarized the goals of both script and production in these competing theatres. As in all generalizations, exceptions will be discovered in both theatres.

Avant-Garde Theatre	Conventional Theatre
Leans toward pessimism, even nihilism; life is considered an absurdity; little hope is held for the individual; the world of the future is even less attractive.	Leans toward optimism; life is considered worth living; hope is held out for the individual; a better world is anticipated.
Finds beauty too mystical, prefers excitement and intuitions; considers truth not absolute and only implied—that the play can be sensually accurate and utterly untrue—finds substance not very important; is more interested in developing a new style and form.	Seeks beauty and truth; finds substance of great importance in defining man and his world; moves in an orderly fashion and accepts established style or form.

Avant-Garde Theatre

Often forgets plot or story; greatly simplifies or symbolizes characters; uses abstract themes; permits dialogue to be formal, simple, or non-existent; is often nonliterary; strives for poetry; reestablishes soliloquy, asides, and chorus or creates similar devices; provides no communication.

Destroys illusion with unrealistic material; seeks to portray the internal; refuses to accept realism as a means of expression; aims at ambiguity; portrays life through broad exaggeration; uses subjective reality.

Accepts obscurity as part of the magic in man's general existence; strives for full theatricality; avoids representation through use of masquerade, circus, dance, ritual, myths as symbols, etc.; appeals to the imagination.

Sees no need for motivation; destroys all illusion; discourages identification.

Creates a strange new structure; is mostly middle, with beginning and end slighted or omitted; accepts no rules for playwriting; has circular plot line (if there is a plot); play often ends as it began.

Abandons realistic settings, eliminating the "fourth wall" (see Glossary); keeps technical effects in full view; always makes the audience conscious it is in the theatre; strives for the illogical, irrational, and unreasonable; places little emphasis on any focus.

Conventional Theatre

Places emphasis on plot or character and a concrete theme; has conversational dialogue; attempts to be literary and is partial to prose; abolishes soliloquy and asides and abandons the chorus; believes man has a "will" and is capable of improving his existence; is capable of communication.

Fosters illusion of reality in imitating life; portrays the external; holds a mirror up to nature; aims for clarity; imitates life's surface; uses objective reality.

Seeks to analyze and understand man's specific problems; would minimize theatricality in the drama; makes performances representational; appeals to the intellect as well as the emotions.

Seeks motivation for action of characters; develops illusion; promotes audience identification with characters.

Accepts some rudiments of structure and rules for playwriting; insists on a beginning, middle, and end; has linear plot line; play progresses to a different conclusion.

Creates realistic settings, including the "fourth wall"; tries to mask technical effects; seeks logic in all things; has order and a central focus.

Avant-Garde Theatre	Conventional Theatre
Abandons aesthetic distance.	Carefully balances empathy and aesthetic distance.
Finds spectacle the most important of the elements of drama.	Finds spectacle the least important of the elements of drama.
Refuses to recognize old aesthetics of drama; chooses stories from symbols, myths, primitive spectacles, medieval farce, and other spectacles; presents situations only representative of life's reality.	Believes in aesthetic drama; chooses stories from imagination, fiction, and history; seeks situations and stories that can be recognized as related to one's existence.
Physically assaults audience or otherwise involves them in the performance; forces breakdown of audience–actor separation in which the whole auditorium becomes the stage.	Encourages audience to enjoy the performance vicariously and through aesthetic distance; retains formal seating and arrangement, with stage and auditorium separated.
Makes no effort to judge morality; has no taboos; insists on utter freedom; is interested in shock values, even to the point of antagonizing the audience.	Has taboos against nudity, unsavory sex, and obscenity; is ever conscious of "good taste" and audience endorsement.
Believes in "art for art's sake" and "theatre for theatre's sake."	Believes in art for "life's sake."

TESTS OF A PLAY'S GREATNESS

We do not say that every play should be great; frequently the dramatist is not even attempting to write a great play. But surely every play must please its audience *now* or it has failed *as theatre*—great as its other values may be. In the theatre, this *of-the-moment* response is of prime importance, for the theatre must capture and hold the immediate interest of its audience and give that audience the maximum pleasure *at that instant*.

In chapter 1 we discussed the journalistic, theatrical, and literary values of scripts. "Greatness" can mean something different under each of these headings. The successful playwright usually has some audience in mind as he begins to work. It may be a very intelligent few, a particular class, a section of the country, or a mass audience. The writer is familiar with an interesting story in this respect.

A well-known American playwright who had a number of successful plays to his credit attended an opening of his new play on its try-out tour. It was a Thursday evening. The audience was very receptive and everything pointed to a successful run. On Friday he did not attend but called the theatre after the performance to inquire about the audience's reaction. He was told that it was even better than the opening night. The Saturday performance was a disappointment. The audience did not accept the serious aspects; they laughed in all the wrong places and failed to get the proper meanings of lines that had seemed very clear on the other nights. When the playwright made his call he was given the bad news—with the explanation that it was "a typical Saturday night audience." The following year this playwright was represented on Broadway by a very light, largely escapist, and highly popular farce that ran well over a year as a continual sell-out. Afterwards it was very successful in the noncommercial theatre. Shortly after the opening, the director of the earlier try-out tour (the play never got to Broadway) was in New York and managed to get a ticket to the new hit. He immediately made a telephone call to the playwright to congratulate him on his success, and was somewhat surprised when the author said: "Well, you are partially responsible for this play. Remember last year when you told me the play didn't go over quite so well on Saturday night? Well, I made up my mind it was just about time I wrote something for that 'Saturday night audience!'" Obviously he had written a theatrical play with "theatre magic," but it was very much dated within less than five years after its New York run.

The best and most recent example of journalistic theatre is the extremely popular and commercially successful *Hair*. It fits perfectly the term "Modcom," a word coined by *Time* magazine, which they define as "the commercial exploitation of modernity without regard for dramatic art." *Time* lists as the rules for this type of production: Be plotless; be lavish with four-letter words; belittle the U.S.A.; mock religions of all kinds; make drug-taking a must; be blatant about sex; deafen the audience; mingle with the audience; condemn Vietnam.

Hair easily meets all these requirements. It has shock value, follows the precepts of Artaud with its ceremonial and ritualistic production numbers, exploits symbolism, and degrades everything that has been held sacred by the audience or the conventional theatre. In the first quarter of an hour—by actual count—it has ridiculed patriotism, religion, parenthood, the flag, education, and everything that is any part of the establishment. Its appeal is to the frustrated masses. It pretends to a sincerity of feeling for the common man, but for anyone who looks deeper than the surface it is purely a commercial venture that has used all the elements of the extreme on the modern scene. This is not to condemn *Hair*, but rather to put it in its proper perspective. It may be "great" for what it tries to be, but its life span will surely be short. The well-known dramatic critic, Norman Nadel, editor of *Critic's Choice,* has written a most interesting history and evaluation entitled: "*Hair*—Progress or Put-On?" With his gracious permission, we present it in full.

" '*HAIR*'—PROGRESS OR PUT-ON?" *

Whatever its merits or demerits, *Hair* has occasioned more discussion than any two or three musicals to have come to Broadway in the past few seasons, and talk almost invariably has been good for the theatre. People have approached it with everything from trepidation to lascivious eagerness, watched with awe, amusement or dismay, and have left the theatre in a state of delight or disgust. Nobody has been indifferent; it is the kind of show about which you just have to choose sides.

Much of the talk has to do with its originality—real or alleged. Unquestionably it is original; nobody can find a single show which its authors might have plagiarized. Still, there is a lot about *Hair* that some of us have seen or heard before, though never in any such combination. And for every claim that it has moved the musical theatre from yesterday to today, there is reason to counter that maybe its effect on this distinctively American art form is retrogressive rather than progressive.

It probably is the only show to have opened three times in New York in the same season, having begun its public life in the fall of 1967, when it opened off-Broadway as a production of the New York Shakespeare Festival—the company headed by Joseph Papp which stages the Bard's comedies and tragedies each summer outdoors in Central Park.

At the time, Gerome Ragni, who co-authored it with James Rado, described *Hair* as "an expression of the hippie philosophy in a very nice way." It also could have been summed up as a four-letter word meaning love, protest, liberation, peace, life, affirmation, permissiveness, sexual freedom, noise, turned-on young people, hippies, pot, brotherhood and joy. Ragni also insisted—and still believes—that *Hair* is not antagonistic or disputatious. "The play is not a putdown of the older generation. The kids (in cast and story) turn people on with love. It is a series of observations of today. There's no plot; we intentionally wrote a non-book, but used elements of the musical theatre. It represents our liberation from racial prejudice, from old religious ideas of sin and guilt feelings, and especially liberation from hate."

Nevertheless, there was a plot of sorts in that earliest, unfinished but rather appealing version. Berger, expelled from school, tells his girl Sheila to spend the night with his friend Claude, who has to go

* "*Hair*—Progress or Put-On?" *Critics Choice* (published by the Theatre Guild), 2, no. 7 (January 15, 1969), 4–5.

into the army. Sheila reluctantly does, to please Berger, which self-sacrifice upsets Jeannie, who loves Claude. There also was a broad caricature of parents and some other social comment, loosely interwoven with this plot (or non-plot).

In time *Hair* completed its limited run downtown, but enough people had faith in it to reopen the show at the Cheetah, a discothèque on Broadway a few blocks above Times Square. This run ended soon after because the building was being torn down—not, however, because *Hair* was in it.

Meanwhile, Michael Butler, the scion of a wealthy Illinois family, had become interested in it to the extent of financing it with a Broadway opening in mind—at one of the legit Broadway theatres, that is. Tom O'Horgan, a young man whose work off-Broadway has been outrageously different and almost unbearably vital, was brought in as director. He gave *Hair* a new and even more disheveled look, and the show's authors, with composer Galt MacDermot, turned out nine more songs.

Somewhere along the line somebody—probably O'Horgan—decided the show needed a touch of nudity, and this variation was hardly kept a secret, so that by opening night the first-nighters were all set to be shocked.

They weren't. At the close of the first act, about five of the girls and young men took off their clothes and stood, jaybird naked, facing the audience. But the theatre was almost dark, except for soft blue lights behind the performers, so the effect was relatively discreet. Nevertheless, that's what the critics and television reviewers mentioned, and that quickly, *Hair* was a hit. There were other elements of interest of course—the jangley, deafening country-rock music, the hippie-type players wandering through the audience handing out flowers, and the fact that the show finally had indeed become a non-plot; that little narrative mentioned a while back had been jettisoned somewhere between the Cheetah and the Biltmore.

Even by opening night, and especially after, some observers were starting to ask if *Hair* was indeed the pioneering project it seemed —if it were an affirmation of love, a credo of liberation and all that —or if it was more a solid hunk of Broadway commercialism, designed to lure the country kin in from the boondocks. Bearing out the latter suspicion was the fact that as time went on, the number of nudies in that first act finale increased, and the soft blue light behind them changed to bright white light smack on them from the front.

Among the many who found this daring and called it original, few bothered to remember the Ziegfeld Follies of 1926, or burlesque, or to hearken back to the Roman Coliseum about two millennia ago, when nude and very literally sexual entertainment was quite as popular as watching the lions snack on religious minorities. Producer Butler, who shortly before had been seen around and about in proper suits, shirts and ties, began appearing in eyeball-shattering mod or hippie outfits, though this could have been mere loyalty to the new creed.

Despite several evidences of what seemed blatant commercialism, the show has maintained a kind of insouciance which most Broadway musicals do not have—and in ordinary instances, do not want. Audiences like this impression of a show put on just because the actors feel like it, though you can be sure that any *Hair* man or maiden who doesn't show up by half-hour call is going to get docked.

As for the non-plot, the disorganization, the thrown-together "happening" aspect; is it the look of the future, or the intentionally discarded look of sloppy theatre in the past? Do we really want to get rid of plot? Is theatre which assails our ears and our eyes—the so-called total theatre—always the most desirable kind? Even if we enjoy *Hair* (and most of us do, in one way or another), would we want much more like it?

Maybe all these questions are irrelevant. The show "works." Whether it is shrill, vulgar, mystical, tender, incomprehensible or silly—and at one time or another it is each of these—it takes the audience out of itself for a little while.

So maybe *Hair*, whether it is commercial, spontaneous or inspirational, has arrived at the right moment. It's still the show New York visitors are curious about. When they go home, whether they complain or praise, at least they talk about the show. And talk is the life blood of *Hair*.

In measuring the work of any artist there are four areas that should always be considered: *imagination, originality, truth,* and *sincerity.* These most important keys will be very helpful as we turn now to some valid tests of a play's greatness as presented by Harold Hobson, London critic; Martin Esslin, foremost authority on the avant-garde; and Joseph Mersand, professor and author.

Harold Hobson has stated that "greatness comes to a play when an intense experience in a fine mind is translated with ecstasy into effective theatrical terms." Mr. Hobson goes on to emphasize that by all odds the most important of these three elements is "theatrical effectiveness" and that without it there is no play, though it is the least literary of the three ingredients. He further points out that with all three we may have an *Othello,* with only the last two we have *The Importance of Being Earnest,* and with only the third we have a *Charley's Aunt.*

Theatrical effectiveness has many degrees. Some plays may send an audience on its way ecstatic with the most enthusiastic approval; others may have pleased in a quieter manner; some may have held the attention in performance and left food for thought in days to come. Still others may have held the attention for the moment, but in the light of the outside world lost much of their lustre. These varying attitudes must be taken into consideration in evaluating any play's true worth.

One ingredient any play must possess is some degree of *universality*. It must concern itself with those basic emotions and fears known to all mankind—anxiety, the fear of being deprived, the suffering of pain or extinction, the need for love and the fear of rejection, the essence of loyalty as contrasted to treason, selfishness versus self-sacrifice, honor versus dishonor, the false as opposed to the true, and good versus evil. In the great plays of the conventional theatre these universals are clearly defined through the picturing of social, economic, psychological, or philosophical conflicts in man's daily contacts and by means of surface realism.

The avant-garde, no longer tied to this exterior presentation, tries to return to the origin of such universals by way of myths and religion, which were the very origin of the theatre itself. Artaud had emphasized the importance of myth. Much of their work is done through symbols. They never speak directly. Their truth lies *behind* the story, and the audience must *search* for that truth. This is one reason the absurd is frowned upon by the lazy spectator, who would prefer not to think or seek out the inner meaning.

Martin Esslin, in his excellent book *The Theatre of the Absurd,* has given us the finest tests of greatness for this new style:

> The Theatre of the Absurd concentrates on the power of stage imagery, on the projection of visions of the world dredged up from the depth of the subconscious. . . . We have to analyze the works themselves and find the tendencies and modes of thought they express, in order to gain a picture of their artistic purpose. And once we have gained a clear idea of their general tendency and aim, we can arrive at a perfectly valid judgment of how they measure up to what they have set out to do. . . . The Theatre of the Absurd is concerned essentially with the evocation of concrete poetic images designed to communicate to the audience the sense of perplexity that their authors feel when confronted with the human condition, and we must judge the success or failure of these works by the degree to which they succeed in communicating this mixture of poetry and grotesque, tragicomic horror. And this in turn will depend on the quality and power of the poetic images evoked. . . .
>
> As in the criticism of poetry, there will always be a subjective element of taste or personal responsiveness to certain associations, but on the whole it is possible to apply objective standards. These standards are based on such elements as (1) *suggestive power,* (2) *originality of invention,* (3) *the psychological truth of the images concerned,* (4) their *depth and universality,* and (5) the *degree of skill with which they are translated into stage terms.**

* Martin Esslin, *The Theatre of the Absurd* (Garden City, N.Y.: Doubleday & Company, Inc., 1969), pp. 367–369.

A number of years ago, Mr. Joseph Mersand compiled five questions for measuring a play's values. For many years these have been the author's guide. After a most careful restudy in the light of what both Mr. Hobson and Mr. Esslin have given us, they seem equally valid today. The tests of any of these three critics would seem to add breadth and depth to those of the other two. We heartily recommend that, with Mr. Hobson's and Mr. Esslin's measures in mind, we also ask Mr. Mersand's five questions for measuring a play's greatness. Does the play:

Possess universality of appeal in time and space?

Create living characters in convincing situations?

Stir, move, enrich, or transform us?

Express its thought in beautiful or appropriate language?

Teach life's meaning and strengthen our own hand in facing life's problems?

Any play worthy of the term "great" must do more than merely hold our interest or entertain us for the moment. It must be really effective in some very definite respect, such as moving us emotionally with its beauty or with its truth, and it must have sufficient strength to sway our thoughts. If it fails here, it is not a great play.

WHAT IS THE DIRECTOR TRYING TO DO?

HOW WELL HAS HE ACCOMPLISHED IT?

THE DIRECTOR'S SUBSTANCE

The drama, itself, as written
The director's interpretation of that drama as it becomes a play

☐ *His tools:* the play, the actors, the technicians, the audience

THE DIRECTOR'S FORM

The choice of play
The casting
The aesthetic style
The audience–actor relationship
The relation of empathy to aesthetic distance

THE DIRECTOR'S TECHNIQUE

How he has emphasized the theme and style of the production
His use of stage movements, business, groupings, and pictures
His emphasis on the whole production
His handling of rhythm, tempo, and pace
His balance of empathy and aesthetic distance
His fidelity to the play's purpose and his materials
The over-all smoothness of the production as measured by the pillars of the fine arts

WAS IT WORTH THE DOING?

THE DIRECTION AND
THE DIRECTOR

DIRECTION: WHAT IT IS

During its long history the theatre has belonged variously to each of its many artists. The playwright, actor, scenic artists, electrician, costumer, and director—each has had "his hour upon the stage." At present the pre-eminent position belongs to the director. It is he who is responsible for the selection, the organization, and the design of the overall production. He is the leader, the coordinator, the guide, the unifier of all the diverse elements that make up the production. Any play that passes through his imagination will have about it something of him.

It was David Garrick, in the mid-eighteenth century, who first began to think of the production as a whole. After him we hear little of the subject until 1874, when the Duke of Saxe-Meiningen established in Germany the idea of the director's discipline over the production. It was his company that influenced the great Stanislavsky in Russia, who incorporated many of Meiningen's ideas in the famous Moscow Art Theatre. There soon emerged in Europe the concept of the *regisseur*, the "artist-director."

Harold Clurman, one of our most capable and sincere directors, has said that the director might be called the author of the stage production. He goes on to say:

"Though the director does not act, he is, or should be, responsible for the kind of acting we see on the stage; though he does not usually design the sets, he is, or should be, responsible for the kind of impression the sets make; and this applies to everything else on the stage." *

Normally the director is the first to receive the script for study and thought. During this period he must discover the *exact* characters of the piece; search out their motives and relationships to each other and to the story; understand just where the play begins, how it builds through a series of crises to a turning point and a climax, and just where the breaks will come. He must discover the mood or atmosphere; in short, he must determine exactly what the "something" is that the playwright has sought.

Once the director has made this discovery and has a full command of the script's substance and form, he must think in terms of actors who will fit into the various roles; of voices and personalities that will blend or contrast properly; of camera movements and pictures; of setting, stage decor, props, lighting, sound, and many other details that will help to interpret and emphasize what he believes the playwright intends. Basically, this is his substance—the material he works with.

In one sense, the director is comparable to the conductor of a symphony orchestra, for, although he is playing no instrument himself, he does unify the work of many individual performers into an artistic whole. He regulates tempo, commands every variation in the emphasis, and creates an interpretation. The director constantly must think of the total effect, for he is the author's representative. It is his responsibility to see that each artist not only suggests a reality that we can believe in so far as the play, the character, and the period represented are concerned, but also that together they *translate, interpret, and express this reality so that it conveys the playwright's attitude.* The attempt to be faithful to this reality involves choices between playing a scene as farce, as high comedy, as melodrama, or as tragedy; between "playing it up," "throwing it away," or "putting it across." It determines the style, the interpretation, and the spirit that the director feels the author had in mind as he wrote the script. In short, it is the director's responsibility to see that the actors and all technicians not only play the characters they have been assigned and furnish the necessary background, but that they also *play the play* that has been written for them. The director endows the written script with the necessary dramatic action and dramatic sound required to project the intellectual and emotional meanings as he interprets them.

Through the *script*, the *actors*, and the *technicians*, he speaks to the *audience*, for these four elements are the director's tools.

* Quoted in John Gassner, *Producing the Play* (The Dryden Press, 1953), p. 273.

THE DIRECTOR'S OBLIGATIONS

TYPES OF THEATRE

Since our premise in artistic evaluation is based on the three principles of Goethe, a director should be measured by the same criteria as the other artists. What are his obligations or goals? What is he trying to do?

Before we can fully answer this question we must point out that the theatre in America today is divided into two general classifications—the "commercial" and the "noncommercial." We have chosen throughout this book to use these terms in preference to "professional" and "amateur" because of the unfortunately derogatory connotation that has come to be associated with the word "amateur" and the ambiguity of "professional" when it applies to any art.

In the theatre the actual distinction between the latter two terms is many times a matter of attitude, and the "amateur" performance, with its high purpose and sincerity, often matches and sometimes excels the work of many so-called "professional" groups. A majority of our summer theatres, a few of our road companies, and an occasional New York production would suffer greatly by any artistic standards when compared to the best work of these noncommercial organizations.

The commercial theatre includes the motion pictures, network television, and those living theatres centered on and off Broadway, as well as the touring organizations that emanate from there. During the summer there are some three to four hundred "straw hat" theatres, many of which are commercial. For the remainder of the year there exist a few regular stock companies and perhaps twenty-five to thirty very promising repertory companies. These all operate under the rules of Actors' Equity Association, the union of professional actors. There are some nonequity companies whose personnel receive moderate salaries, with the financing provided solely by the box office. They are, therefore, classified as commercial companies.

The noncommercial theatre is divided roughly into two classifications —community theatre and educational theatre. The first includes approximately two-hundred-fifty top flight organizations (some with a record of forty or fifty years of continuous operation) and literally hundreds of groups that produce occasionally but not on a regular schedule. In addition there are thousands of church, fraternal, civic, and art drama groups that operate sporadically.

The educational theatre includes high school, college, and university dramatic programs, all of which are related to and underwritten by the institutions of which they are a part. Drama was introduced into colleges in 1899 at Columbia University when Brander Matthews became the first professor of a dramatics class in an English-speaking university. Its growth has been phenomenal since that date, and the United States leads the world in its recognition of the theatre as an educational medium.

Every good director, regardless of the organization he represents, realizes there is only one standard of excellence in theatre art. He will not try to excuse the less-than-successful production by rationalizations of any kind. He knows that the inexperienced participants in an educational or community theatre may not come as close to scaling the artistic heights of a commercial company, but the first goal of each and every dramatic production should be the same—*a complete artistic success!*

In addition to this major obligation, every director should challenge both audience and participants in a manner that will broaden their dramatic horizons but not out-distance their understanding, for, as a director, it is his duty always to keep the theatre both popular and alive.

Every director has certain obligations to the playwright whose script he is interpreting as well as to the play itself. Each is deserving of a sincere, artistic, and faithful production.

These are obligations common to every director, regardless of the theatre in which he works. In addition, the commercial, community, and educational theatres all have their own separate goals, and each individual theatre has its own local needs. Unless we have given some thought to all these demands we have not been wholly honest in our evaluation of the director's work.

In the commercial theatre and motion pictures the director must attract to the box office a sufficient audience to pay all production costs and running expenses with some margin of profit for those who have underwritten the production. In addition, he hopes to win the approval of a large number of playgoers and the commendation of professional dramatic critics.

Although many of us feel that the commercial theatre often falls short of its obligation as an art form, we should constantly remind ourselves that it is also a profession and a business and as such the economic element is inextricably interwoven with the artistic. Realizing this, we may be a little less prone to dismiss a production as mere "show business." Theatre workers must eat and theatre producers must live, and the commercial theatre is obligated to give the audience what it will buy. In the novel *The Devil's Profession,* by Russell O'Neil, one of the characters makes a statement that has a great deal of validity:

Commercialism may not be entirely desirable in the theatre, but neither is pseudo-intellectual isolationism. There are those who turn their backs on the harsh reality of the public taste and indulge themselves in meaningless mumbo-jumbo under the gallant banner of avant-gardism, or the guise of "raising the level of public taste." These would-be reformers do not realize that such a goal cannot be accomplished by forcing on the public their own standards, or their own philosophy of art—particularly when there is no evidence that theirs is any better. No man has the right to say that this the public should see and this it should not. This would be a form of artistic fascism which is dangerous and should be deplored far more than commercialism. It is smug and theatre smugness can only breed stagnation.*

Television also is a business as well as an art, but here there is an additional factor, for it must sell something besides itself. Only by the grace of the advertiser do we have a program at all. For this reason we must accept the commercial as inevitable, even though it does break the continuity of the story, and reduce its total effectiveness by forcing in extraneous materials. Since we rarely consider the cost and upkeep of the set itself, our admission is measured by the minutes we give the sponsor. Certainly this is small enough payment for some of the fine dramatic entertainment available.

In contrast to this commercialization of an art, the community theatres are usually organized not for the purpose of making money but to satisfy the creative desires of their members, to answer the frequent question of what to do with leisure time, and to bring together people in a community or group who have the same artistic interests. The community theatre, interested as it is in the artistic success of its productions and in balancing its budget, exists also as a creative and social organization for the benefit of its members and its audience.

Any director who serves such a theatre is responsible to his organization for fulfilling these additional goals. They are not only justified, but are a vital part of the organization itself. Every member of the audience has a right to demand as fine an example of theatre as this group can give, but in his criticism he must not forget that the community theatre does have further commitments of its own.

In both the community and the educational theatre the director must be ever cognizant of those obligations common to all directors: a completely artistic production, a challenge to both participants and audience, and a conscientious loyalty to the script and the playwright himself. These two theatres have an additional obligation in common—that of bringing the living theatre to an audience that has no other opportunity

* Russell O'Neil, *The Devil's Profession* (New York: Simon & Schuster Inc., 1964), pp. 65–66.

for such an experience, for many times these groups furnish the only source of live theatre to their communities. The educational theatre, particularly, must serve as a teacher if it is to justify its existence as part of the institution it represents. As such it possesses a special duty to the students who will attend the performances. The educational theatre director must give that group an introduction to and eventually an appreciation of the best in dramatic literature as well as good theatre. In addition, he has a further obligation to the individual student who wishes to work in any phase of the dramatic program. The *desire* must, of course, be accompanied by sufficient *talent* and *ability*, but those students who possess these three important qualifications must each be given an equal opportunity to participate on a strictly competitive basis. This can eliminate what is known as type-casting. To take its place there is a method far superior both for the training of actors and for the future of the theatre, and this is a compromise between type-casting and miscasting. This approach permits a greater number of students to participate. Type-cast productions, on the other hand, tend to use the same actors over and over again. The same is true in all other areas of the theatre—carpentry, costuming, make-up, lighting, painting, designing, and writing. Truly, in the educational theatre lies a gigantic opportunity to teach cooperation, teamwork, loyalty, and responsibility. Nowhere is each better realized than in the well-rounded dramatic production. The educational theatre director holds in his hands the great opportunity to help his students to develop physically, vocally, intellectually, emotionally, culturally, and socially.

The director also has an obligation to the educational system and to the theatre as an institution that the plays selected should represent not only the best in type, style, and structure, but that they should come from every period of dramatic literature. His program should represent a sort of living library. At the same time, he must not reach beyond the comprehension of the students involved or the audience that he will attract. They must be challenged, but failure to meet the challenge can not only harm the participants but disappoint and lose the audience as well. The choice of the play is of vital importance in every way. It must attract the audience as well as appeal to it after it is there. It has always been necessary for the theatre to create its audience. Today, if the stage is to survive, this must be accomplished by the directors in community and educational theatres. A theatre program that is too heavy can prove disastrous. It must begin with more popular dramatic material. The director must know his audience and must furnish it with a variety of plays that represent all types and styles of drama (as discussed in chapter 2). Failing to follow such a plan can only result in empty seats, dissatisfaction on the part of cast and staff, and the loss of a potential audience.

Nor is this learning process ever complete, for each September brings to the campus a new group, and the process must begin again. A director in an educational theatre should not be judged on the choice of a single play or a single season. The programs can be fairly evaluated only by considering three or four consecutive seasons or whatever number comprises the student generation.

Finally, there is the ever important and not-to-be-forgotten obligation to the theatre director himself. He must satisfy his own artistic as well as educational standards. This can be done only after he has first considered positively the other demands, although at times it may be necessary to compromise here and there in order to give the most to the greatest number. Only in meeting the first four obligations can he as a director in the educational theatre meet the fifth, that of satisfying himself.

The director in the noncommercial theatre—community or educational—has five distinct obligations beyond bringing the best in live theatre to his audience and presenting an artistic production faithful to the author's script. These obligations are:

To entertain and educate the audience and also to build an audience for the theatre of the future.

To develop the talents and further the creativity of those participants actively involved in the production.

To further the aims of the particular organization he represents.

To contribute artistically to the theatre as an institution and an art.

To satisfy himself as a director, an artist, and a teacher.

Directors in countless noncommercial theatres throughout America are meeting these obligations most successfully. These organizations are the living stage's greatest hope for the future. The creed of one university theatre summarizes so well what many educational and community theatres are trying to do that it is reproduced here in its entirety.

Our Theatre shall endeavor always:

To develop its students as individuals—vocally, physically, emotionally, and culturally—rather than for the commercial theatre

To train both audience and students to appreciate the living theatre

To present plays that picture all phases of life and dramatic literature

To approach perfection in its own realm without attempting to imitate Broadway

To encourage creative work in every phase of the dramatic arts

To add stature to the theatre in general, and to the college theatre in particular

To be always *educational, challenging,* and *artistic!**

We must not dwell over-long on this subject, but if each noncommercial theatre and its director is to receive the same honest critical evaluation that we would ask for all artists, its is necessary that some of the particular problems and specific goals be understood by the critic.

SUBSTANCE

The director's substance is the script itself and his interpretation of that script as it is brought to life in the theatre. This involves what he wants it to say to the audience as well as what he feels the author meant it to say. He may change the period, the style, even the type. There are many opinions as to just how much license a director really has. Some contend that the moment the printed script becomes a play it has entered a new medium and that the director is as creative as the playwright who wrote it. There are others who feel that a script should not be altered but should be interpreted exactly as the author intended, or as nearly as possible. We will neither enter into this controversy nor voice an opinion of it. We are primarily interested at the moment in what the director has tried to do.

DEFINITION

To clarify these all-important obligations we now present our preferred definition of the role of the director:

> *It is the duty of the director to create the complete and accurate theatrical effect demanded by the play's type, style, spirit, and purpose, and to project this creation through such visual and auditory stimuli as will produce in the audience a definite emotional and/or intellectual impression.*

It has been wisely said also that the director decides *what* is to be done, and his fellow artists—the actors and technicians—are responsible for *how* the *what* is accomplished. The director, actors, and technicians can each find ample room for individual freedom of expression and interpretation within the confines of the "what" and "how." The work of the actors and technicians will be discussed in later chapters. We

* The Departmental Creed: Denison University, Granville, Ohio, 1939.

now consider the director's contributions to the fulfillment of the above requirements.

THE DIRECTOR'S FORM

One of the first items to be considered here must be the actual choice of play. Here the responsibility in the noncommercial field is greater than in the commercial theatre. In the latter, a director is hired to direct a particular play and can be held responsible for its selection only in that he did accept the assignment. If the play is wholly unworthy, then he, as well as the producer, may be justly criticized.

In the community and educational theatre every organization in each city or community calls for its own individual program of plays. The fact that a play was successful in New York does not mean that it is a great play, and by the same token, that a play fails in New York or has not played there is no indication that it is a poor play. The great hit of 1960 may or may not be right for a theatre in 1975. The types of theatre demanded by the audiences in a metropolitan center, on a midwestern college campus, and in a Texas community theatre are not at all the same. Locale and time are both involved in the choice of a play that will attract an audience and do the most for it and the theatre at any given time or place. Audiences are often not ready for a particular play. To misjudge the temperament, desire, or understanding of the potential audience in any locality is only to ask for empty seats or an unenthusiastic audience; both are harmful equally to the theatre and to the producing group.

Producers in the professional theatre do sometimes insist upon special friends for certain roles, and actors have been known to produce plays only so that they could play coveted parts, even though they were not equipped to do them well. Nevertheless, the province of casting is normally considered to be the director's. He may choose to type-cast and thus make his production easier to direct and more believable to the audience. On the other hand, he may choose to develop someone in a role, altering the actor's appearance by the use of make-up. This is usually a necessity in the educational theatre, where there are only young actors to play the mature roles.

The element of interpretations is also important. The director must decide on the demands of the role. With thousands of actors—good ones—begging for parts, it is not unusual to read that the production of a play has been postponed because the director was unable to cast it. As an illustration, let us suppose a playwright has pictured a specific character as shy, retiring, bashful, reluctant to speak up and express himself. Such a character could be interpreted by the director in any of several ways, each accompanied by all the shadings of a human personality. The character could arouse a warm sympathy by his quaint, shy, and lovable quality; he could become a broad comedy character at whom the audience could laugh boisterously; or he could be a stupid individual whom the audience might prefer to boot right off the stage. Each could be a logical interpretation.

Harold Clurman put it another way when he said that the whole meaning of the play *Golden Boy*, by Clifford Odets, depended upon whether the director saw the leading character, Joe Bonaparte, as a fighter who had a gift for music, or as a musician who had a gift for fighting. Each is a matter of interpretation.

Allied to the choice of the play and the casting, most directors in the noncommercial theatre face a special problem. They often have a limited number of capable actors. This can limit the choice of program, since Shaw, Chekhov, Pirandello, Shakespeare, Sophocles, Molière, Corneille, and even many of our present-day writers make some rather extravagant demands of the actor. It would be unwise to choose a play —great though it may be—for which an adequate cast could not be found. Directors often err in this respect. Bernard Shaw's admonition was, as usual, sage: "You must not keep on confusing the appreciation and understanding of parts and plays with the ability to act them."

We would emphasize that good theatre—regardless of the period it represents—can be exciting, but only if it is well done. The television and motion-picture fields have been very careful in this respect, and they have the distinct advantage of both unlimited talent and apparently unlimited funds to pay for it. If the stage is to attract the new audience that is now accustomed only to motion pictures and television, its productions must be equally exciting. The director who constantly strives to uplift the stage in the face of such competition is to be commended, but as a wise theatre man once said: "We are all for elevating the stage, but those of us who love the legitimate theatre would not suggest doing it by depressing the audience."

ACTOR AND AUDIENCE RELATIONSHIP

One of the earliest and most fundamental decisions the actor and director must make for each production is whether the actor's performance will be audience-centered (presentational) or stage-centered (representational). Will it be nonillusionistic (no attempt to give the impression that these events are actually occurring) or illusionistic (these lines and these emotions are all very real; the characters mean what they say and do; the events are actually happening). Although the playwright's script may suggest the proper approach, it is the director's decision that makes it evident to the audience.

In the theatre of the Greeks, Shakespeare, Molière, the Restoration, and of the eighteenth and nineteenth centuries, the form was essentially audience-centered. The large audience, outdoor performances, and aesthetic styles of all these periods made it practically mandatory. The play was presented straight *to* the audience, almost as if the audience were another character in the drama—a character without lines to speak. The audience, in effect, was taken into the confidence of the actors. Such information as it should have was given out directly by the chorus, or through a soliloquy, or, later, by an aside. This form is common today in the television skit in which two comedians engage in a verbal feud with each other while directing their lines to the audience. We call this *presentational theatre.* The old melodrama, in which the villain walked down to the footlights and confided his thoughts to the audience, was an exaggeration of this form. This presentational approach is used in many avant-garde productions.

Presentational drama can be either illusionistic or nonillusionistic. Certainly the actors in the roles of Oedipus, Electra, Agamemnon, Hamlet, Macbeth, King Lear, and even Tartuffe intend that the audience should believe what they see and should receive the impression that this situation actually exists and that the emotions and incidents are all very real. These plays are, then, presentational and illusionistic. This same technique—presentational and illusionistic—is used by the monologuist—Cornelia Otis Skinner, for example, and the late Ruth Draper in their one-woman shows, or Hal Holbrook in his remarkable performance in *Mark Twain Tonight!*

On the other hand, many comedies, such as *The Rivals* and *She Stoops to Conquer,* and much of the eighteenth- and nineteenth-century sentimental drama might easily have been meant to give the impression that a group of actors—rather than characters—is telling a story. Each actor takes on the vocal and physical characteristics of the character he portrays, but he, the actor, is always present. It is almost as if he is speaking in the third person. This treatment is called "presentational" and is nonillusionistic. This is the approach desired by Brecht and much of the absurdist theatre.

When the theatre moved indoors the scenic background became more realistic, the lighting improved (and with it the intimacy of the production), and there was greater effort to give the impression of reality. The style developed more and more toward realism or naturalism, and thus the stage-centered production came into existence. The audience ceased to receive the direct attention of the actors. The actors spoke only to each other. Their lines were intended for the audience instead of directed at it. Eventually, an imaginary "fourth wall" was erected and the audience figuratively looked through that wall at the actors. The actor's goal was to make the audience believe he was the character he pretended to be and that the story was actually occurring.

Plays can be ruined because the actors have not understood, mastered, or settled on a consistent approach to the actor-audience relationship. An ultrarealistic, modern play that depends upon the audience's belief and empathic response could have its very point shattered if one of the actors were suddenly to step out of the illusionistic and stage-centered form and make a speech directly to the audience.

Interpretation, spirit, intent, director's and actor's goals, the playwright's purpose—all these help to dictate exactly how the director will conceive the actor's role in respect to his audience. For our purpose it is necessary only that we understand the meaning of these terms so that we can judge more accurately what the director is trying to do insofar as the actor-audience relationship is concerned.

EMPATHY AND AESTHETIC DISTANCE

The type, style, spirit, and purpose of the play determine how much empathy and how much aesthetic distance is demanded. The determination of aesthetic distance is the job of each artist involved, but most especially of the director. The balance between empathy and aesthetic distance is one of the most important aspects of any theatre production.

We have seen how the various playwrights of the nonconventional theatre use these two devices. Pirandello, Sartre, and especially Pinter lean more heavily toward the demands of the conventional theatre. Brecht, with his desire for alienation and detachment, requires a great deal of aesthetic distance. An empathic production strives for "psychological truth" through emotion. Brecht preferred "social truth," developed through the intellect. Artaud disdains all aesthetic distance and encourages a maximum of empathy. Beckett demands a strange combination that puts the spectators into a kind of camaraderie with the characters on stage yet produces in them a sense of absurdity and monotony. Ionesco desires little empathy. This pattern, of course, varies to some degree with every production.

The demands of the conventional theatre have, similarly, varied through the years. Aesthetic distance in the Greek and Shakespearean theatres was largely sustained by the language and the nobility of the characters and their more formal presentation. During the Restoration in England aesthetic distance and empathy were both made more difficult for the general audience because some of the privileged spectators sat on the stage—where they participated in the action by responding to the actors' lines and injecting their own remarks into the production.

In the eighteenth and nineteenth centuries actors remained clearly actors and audiences appraised them and their art as individuals. Aesthetic distance predominated in these performances as audiences thought in terms of the individual's actor's interpretation and artistry rather than of the character he was portraying.

Today much of the criticism we hear of the arena stage comes from those who are distracted by the proximity of the actors or by the spectators who can be seen on the opposite side of the playing area. This serves to to hinder a full empathic response, but can be destructive of aesthetic distance as well.

There are those who want to "put the play in the lap of the audience." Olson and Johnson did this with their highly popular and strictly escapist *Hellzapoppin* long before Artaud's influence was felt. The entire auditorium has been used as an acting area, with aisles used for entrances, and yet both aesthetic distance and empathy have been sustained because the actor remained a part of the play and never embarrassed individuals in the audience by involving them in its action. Max Reinhardt attained this most successfully in *The Miracle*.

Of the more conventional types of theatre, melodrama requires the greatest empathy. Its loosely drawn characters permit the audience greater leeway in self identification, and the very nature of the situations carries a greater emotional impact. Of the four play types, the least empathy is desired in farce, for here the spectator never wishes to identify with the situation observed. To be actually involved in such circumstances would be unpleasant, but to observe them happening to someone else gives the audience a detachment which, coupled with a feeling of superiority, brings about the unrestrained laughter that we associate with farce. In emotional comedy, where we become personally interested in the outcome of the conflict, the need is for more empathy. In the intellectual comedy, where the outcome is of less interest than the tactics used, aesthetic distance is more to be desired.

Undoubtedly the Greeks found greater empathy in their tragedies than we can sense today, for they were an essential part of their religion and daily life, while we view them as works of art. In the same sense we are rarely caught up empathically at a production of *Hamlet*, much as we may be stirred emotionally and aesthetically by its beauty and its power.

Every play, conventional or avant-garde, if it is to accomplish its purpose, must happen *in* the audience empathically or aesthetically. The degree will depend on the play's substance, purpose, and total goal. The accomplishment of that degree involves not only the selection and arrangement, but the all-important problem of being just real enough to look *like* life and unreal enough not to *be* life, but sufficiently real to picture the reality desired by playwright and director.

After the performance we—as intelligent spectators—should recognize the artistry with which this balance has been accomplished.

THE DIRECTOR'S TECHNIQUE

EMPHASIS ~ SPIRIT ~ PERSONAL STYLE

How a director has managed to emphasize the theme and style of his production should be observed and appreciated. There are directors whose greatest ability lies in serious drama and tragedy and others who find their strength in comedy and farce. While it is generally agreed that few directors can make a poor play seem great, it has been proved over and over again that a good director can improve on a poor script. It is also possible that he may not have done as well by the script as it deserved. Many a fine play has been ruined in the hands of an incompetent director.

No two directors can possibly give the same total effect, even if they have been assigned identical casts and staging. A director's particular style is always there, evident in shadings of meaning, changes in emphasis, interpretation, characterization, and movement. He determines the spirit and purpose of the production.

Each director may place a slightly different emphasis on the theme as the author has expressed it. He may even point up one of his own that will make the play infinitely more timely and appropriate. This was done effectively by Orson Welles in his New York production of *Julius Caesar* during the peak of Mussolini's power. By emphasizing the dangers inherent in dictatorships and staging the play in a modern style, with the conspirators in black shirts, Welles gave the whole production an exciting, timely, new meaning.

In such instances a play may owe more to its director than its author. Peter Brook's A *Midsummer Night's Dream* proved to be more Brook than Shakespeare. Any production by Elia Kazan obviously bears his touch. Margaret Webster is always completely honest in her interpretations of Shakespeare, but they all carry the colorful, pictorial contributions that belong to Miss Webster. The director is even more important in motion pictures. Moviegoers would oftentimes be surer of artistic productions if they chose their pictures by the director rather than the actors.

Some directors prefer to do Shakespeare in modern dress. *Hamlet* has been seen with Ophelia drunk instead of insane and Hamlet in a tuxedo smoking a cigarette. Recently he was played in boxer shorts. In *The Taming of the Shrew*, Petruchio has arrived on a donkey, on horseback, on a motorcycle, and in a battered old jalopy. Directors may choose to "camp" or "kid" a production, to treat it as "artistic child's play," to burlesque it, to do it as a period piece or modernized, as "tongue-in-cheek" or in complete sincerity, for "real" or as "make-believe." All of these approaches show the director's personal style. The spirit of the production is limited only by the director's imagination.

We must always ask if every actor is playing in the same key. If not, the director is at fault. In one production of Othello the whole play lost its effect because Othello used all the gusto of the romantic style, accompanied by the rant of declamation while Iago was played in a completely realistic manner. This error is more common in the non-commercial theatre because of the variety of styles and techniques that appear in nonprofessional casts.

The word "action" in the theatre denotes only the dramatic action of the play that is inherent in the lines and story. Change of position on the stage is called "movement." "Business" includes bodily gesture and the handling of props. While both business and movement may be devised by the actors, the director is responsible, if only for having permitted them. Therefore we may hold the actor responsible for the ease and truth of the execution of movements and bits of business, but whether they distract from or add to the scene or character is dependent upon the director. Again, the "what" and the "how."

The director must always be responsible for furniture arrangement, which will, of course, do much in determining stage groupings, which must always be the director's work. The famous director and teacher Alexander Dean often said to his actors: "You are the hands of the clock up there on the stage, but I am out here where I can tell the time." Stage groupings are of great importance. They must take into consideration the sight lines in the auditorium, so that every important gesture can be seen by all the audience. They must show the different physical and psychological relationships as the play progresses. The stage must always reveal the balance, emphasis, variety, and dramatic meaning necessary to help carry the story, as well as present an agreeable picture every moment. The stage is a continuously changing picture, but there must always be a focal point. Every movement and every bit of business must have a reason and a specific purpose.

The question of under-acting or over-acting may be considered largely in the director's domain. Contrary to the commonly accepted belief, the noncommercial theatre is more likely to under-act and the professional to over-act. The director must have toned up or toned down as the demand required. It is in this area that many directors come in for their most severe criticism, for they think of themselves as creators in their own right rather than as interpreters of the author's script. A director may have a special flair for creating stage business, ingenious ideas of interpretation, or other embellishments through which he thrusts upon a play more of himself and his own abilities than are good for the production. Worthington Miner has said:

> If a director with a formula chooses a good play and attempts to apply the formula to it, he cheats the play and the author. The star director works for his star, the clever director and the director with a theory work for themselves, or sometimes . . . for something extraneous to the play. A conscientious director in normal circumstances works and can work only for the play.*

There is always the possibility that a cast too long away from the director may allow to creep into the play business and line readings that were not a part of the original direction. This frequently occurs with touring productions and especially in noncommercial theatre, where the actors do not possess the technique and discipline to assure the same performance night after night. Actors stretch out their laughs or prolong and continue to enlarge the pantomime that appeals to the audience; in other words, they ham it up. Such an actor is soon attracting more attention to himself and to his performance than to the play. This often happens in long runs of a professional production. There is an old story of a notice that appeared on a theatre callboard several weeks after the opening:

Rehearsal Call—11:00 A.M. Monday

"To take out the improvements"

—*George M. Cohan*

The director should be primarily interested in the play as a whole rather than in the separate parts, in scenes rather than in particular lines, in the overall stage picture rather than in the individual actors. His job is to give the complete meaning and mood of the play and the changing relationships of each character to the play and to each other. Though he may have to work with individuals, he must think in terms of the whole rather than the parts. He must strive for teamwork and unity in the full interpretation of the script. The audience is not conscious of individual bits or lines or characterizations. It feels and thinks in terms of scenes and meanings, crises, themes, and a unity of the whole.

If the author has not made all points perfectly clear, it is the director

---

* Quoted in John Gassner, *Producing the Play* (New York: The Dryden Press, 1953), pp. 210–11.

who must clarify and emphasize these details in his production. He may do so with movement, line, color, mass, force, or any other attribute he may choose. He is a translator who uses all the arts of the theatre to correct any weakness inherent in the script. He has the final task of making everything clear.

RHYTHM ~ TEMPO ~ PACE

There are three concepts that have oftentimes proved to be the greatest pitfall of the noncommercial theatre and the most difficult aspect of a play to explain; they provide, perhaps the greatest single distinction between the experienced and inexperienced worker in the theatre. They are *rhythm, tempo,* and *pace*. These elements, when they are absolutely right, will cover a multitude of other sins and they are the director's responsibility.

"Rhythm" is defined as the recurrence of an accented beat. Its place in music is easily established and understood. It is quite different in the theatre, because not only does theatre employ a broken rhythm, but that rhythm comes from many different sources. The emphasis of a word is, of course, important and easily recognized, but emphasis may also come from the entrance or exit of a character, the audience's sudden awareness of some change within a character, the use of a light, an off-stage noise, a brightly colored costume, the gesture or movement of an actor, and many times—especially in comedy or farce—in an audience reaction.

The rhythm of a play is established very early and remains basically the same throughout the performance, although it may grow in intensity. The "tempo" alters—though the change may be ever so slight—with the entrance or exit of every character, many times within a scene, and constantly during the evening. The director who senses that a play seems to be running slowly and calls out: "Speed it up!" is utterly lacking in any knowledge of rhythm, tempo, and pace and their delicate balance. To speed up a scene is merely to talk faster, to "railroad it" as it is called in the theatre, and all that happens is that the scene gets over more quickly. This, however, is the most frequent criticism of the untrained critic in the audience who proclaims: "The play was slow," "It seemed to drag," "The actors talked too fast," or "They didn't pick up their cues." All these are logical criticisms and may have been true, but the real fault is more basic. The chances are much more likely that the director had failed to point up a defined rhythm or discover the correct pace.

"Pace" is the relationship between the basic rhythm and the ever-changing tempo. It is also the speed of the play *as it seems to an audience.* It comes from the rapidity with which the audience receives a new impulse of interest through the introduction of new ideas or awareness of character development or change in the stage situation. It is at its best when the whole production gives the impression of complete smoothness and authority. Strangely enough, the director finds his success in this respect easier with serious plays. This is largely because he can foresee the audience reaction in drama more easily than in comedy or farce. At least the reaction to drama is more constant.

Comedy, and to an even greater extent farce, are most difficult to do successfully with an inexperienced cast. The comedy lines of the playwright receive such varied reactions from the audience that the actors must constantly cope with those changes and still maintain the rhythm, tempo, and pace that the performance demands. The actors must alter their readings of lines and their actions within a single performance if they are to reestablish the rhythm as it was set by the director in rehearsals. If something unforeseen occurs on stage to alter that rhythm and pace, or the audience contributes a new beat through an unscheduled laugh or other reaction, or fails to supply the one that had been expected, it is only the actors who can once more get the play back on the right track. It is this combination of audience reaction and the actors' recognition of it that can make a comedy so much more satisfying on the stage than in either motion pictures or television.

Rouben Mamoulian, famous motion-picture and New York theatre director, often establishes a rhythm through the use of a rocking chair, a metronome, or some similar device. He and others have been known to direct plays from out front with a baton. The pace of a performance and its integral parts are definitely in the province of the director, although his work is sometimes almost lost in the hands of an inept cast or because of the unexpected response of an audience. It is, nevertheless, part of the critic's task to ascertain what the director has tried to do with these intangibles of dramatic production.

FIDELITY TO SCRIPT AND MATERIALS

It is no small part of the director's responsibility to understand the basic reason for the play's existence—that is, what the playwright was trying to say or do. Once he does understand this, he must then do all he can to emphasize these goals through his direction. There must be a fidelity to the central idea. All the artists must subordinate any personal desire to elaborate upon their work by including some personal talent or preoccupation. Even the playwright may have been guilty in this respect, and if this is true, it is the director's duty to handle the situation or scene so that it will not detract from the overall meaning.

A most striking illustration comes from *The Cocktail Party,* by T. S. Eliot. This play proved an enigma to many theatregoers in both England and America. The lack of clarity was partially due to a scene in the second act just after the psychiatrist had convinced a young lady that she should abandon the immoral life she was living and pay penance for her sins by joining the missionaries in some foreign country. After her exit, the psychiatrist, and his wife and secretary drink a toast to their accomplishment, but the lines do not indicate either the sincerity or the seriousness we have associated with the characters. It is this scene that has been one of the most difficult to rationalize in terms of the remainder of the play. An unquestioned authority has reported that Mr. Eliot was repeatedly advised to delete this entire scene and that he even admitted it had no particular place in the drama, but added: "It is the sort of thing I do so well."

Every artist could make the same excuse for embellishing his work, but such embellishments only serve to cloud the main issue. It is the director's responsibility to keep a strong hand on the reins, and since he has the final authority as to what will be seen and heard, he must possess a greater integrity and artistic sense than any of the others; he, too, has "the sort of thing he does so well." Every artist should show a fidelity to his materials, and the director once more must take the responsibility for it. There are natural limitations to every art. Each artist must recognize and abide by them. He should not try to make a play look like a motion picture, an extravaganza, or a musical. He must not attempt to make the play designed as mere escape pass as a play of social significance. If he wants to present a solution to some personal problem, he should not make it appear greater than it actually is. If the play's chief emotion is only sentimentality, then that should be expressed as sincerely as possible.

The artist–director must resist the temptation to borrow from the other arts and use beautiful costumes, settings, lighting, and music only because they *are* beautiful rather than because they help to emphasize his central idea. No artist must more consistently question himself than the director, and these questions, if honestly answered, will always take him back to the meaning and purpose of the play and whether or not he projects them clearly and with the maximum but honest use of his materials.

PILLARS OF THE FINE ARTS

We should have become aware already of the director's conception of the total production: its originality, truth, imagination, and sincerity. All four are hopefully present to some degree in each of the arts involved. Their implementation is achieved and projected through the production by means of its unity, emphasis, rhythm, balance, proportion, harmony, and grace. In our explanations of these terms we emphasize that, though each does possess a special meaning of its own, there is an inevitable overlapping.

"Unity," as the word implies, is a oneness, a singleness of purpose. It would be absurd to place eighteenth-century costumes in front of a realistic setting. If a director proposes to do Shakespeare in modern dress, he must have sufficient imagination to convey the mood throughout the whole production. Costuming and scenery must suggest the same spirit. All acting should be in the same style, and that style should fit the spoken lines. Periods should not be mixed, nor should the voices or heights of actors be too divergent. A central idea or theme should be underlined in every way possible. Moods or emotions, although appropriately varied, should be in the same general key. The whole production should have what Plato called "unity in variety."

"Emphasis" is a pointing up or stressing of important points, a singling out of that which is most vital. It may be accomplished by movement, line, mass, color, force, or any other means the artist may wish to employ. Unity and emphasis together afford the most effective means of eliminating both distraction and monotony, the two enemies of attention. In so doing they bring into focus what we call primary (or involuntary) attention—that which we give automatically and without any effort whatsoever. Its counterpart is secondary (or voluntary) attention to which we must force ourselves. The theatre must always command involuntary attention only.

"Rhythm," as we have already said, is the recurrence of the accented beat. We are all creatures of rhythm throughout our lives. It is constantly a part of us; it is in our breathing, the beating of our hearts, the days of the week, the seasons of the year. In the theatre we become more conscious of rhythm when it is interrupted than we are when it is there. A fluffed line, an awkward pause, a break in the flow of the play, too long a wait for an audience reaction makes one suddenly aware that something has gone wrong. It is this element of rhythm that makes a comedy so much more difficult to play than a serious play, for the overt reaction of those out front becomes a part of the overall rhythm, and that may change—if ever so slightly—from performance to performance. Actors must constantly be making adjustments to audience reaction.

"Balance" and "Proportion" are so closely related that it is difficult to make a distinction. They both indicate an equalizing of forces one against the other. Although it is not wholly true, we do sometimes—at least in the theatre—think of balance as being more visual and proportion as a less tangible relationship. Using this connotation, we might consider "balance" to relate to the stage setting and furniture arrangement, the symmetry and use of line, mass, and color in decor.

"Proportion" may then be considered to be the relation of theme to plot, music to story, the relation between the two contending forces in the play's conflict, and so forth. The old melodramas, for example, fail in proportion because they "stacked the cards" against the villain and in favor of the hero or heroine. Plays have been thrown completely out of focus when a leading actor was far superior to the remainder of the cast. The wise director, therefore, may not permit an actor to give his most brilliant performance if the player opposite him is unable to rise to that height. The director must also balance the work of all the technicians. If the audience remembers settings, lights, or costumes at the expense of the play, the proportion has been faulty.

"Harmony" is a term with which we are all familiar. In the theatre it is the happy and smooth coordination of all phases of production so that nothing interferes with the basic meaning and purpose of the play. It is the ultimate objective of the artistic dramatic production.

"Grace" implies a minimum of effort. It is the ease and facility with which the artist executes his work and thus masks his technique.

SUMMARY

Finally, the director in our modern theatre is responsible for every phase of the production. It is he who determines the emphasis, spirit, and mood; the pointing up of some speech or business and the down playing of others; the balancing of forces and characters; the elimination of distractions, simplification of lines or action that are not wholly clear; the unification of the contributions of all the technicians; the control of the rhythm, tempo, and pace and the fresh, restrained, easy, and convincing quality of the total production.

The alert theatregoer may come to recognize the technique of a given director, just as the connoisseur of art knows at a glance the work of a great painter and the trained musician can recognize, after a few bars, the music of a well-known composer. The artists work alone, each striving for his own unity, emphasis, rhythm, balance, proportion, harmony, and grace. The director, too, seeks all these qualities, but he must achieve them by harmonizing the work of all the other artists.

In summary, we should look for the director's form and technique, the sum total of his artistry, in:

His choice of script, in accordance with the goals of the organization he represents and in accordance with both the group's potentialities and his own.

His casting of the play, with some consideration of the same limitations described above.

His balance of theatricalism and reality, with full recognition of the script's needs.

His treatment of the play's type, with the proper touch breadth or subtlety.

His choice and handling of both the play's aesthetic style and his own particular style.

His projection of the spirit and purpose of whatever play he feels is best suited to a particular time, a particular locale, and a particular audience.

His own balancing of empathy and aesthetic distance and how it is projected through the audience-actor relationship, staging, groupings, picturization, decor, lighting, costuming, and all other visual and auditory stimuli.

His coordination of these many elements and the combined work of all contributing artists to bring about a completely unified production with the maximum harmony and consummate grace.

Only through recognition of what the director has tried to do and the extent to which he has succeeded or failed are we able to appreciate his form and his technique—his contributions and merit as an artist.

There are many fine directors in the theatre today. Brecht's concept of alienation has had a great effect on our stage. The refined artistry of the late Tyrone Guthrie has left its imprint. Several young directors in England, notably Peter Brook with his concept of "total theatre," have had a tremendous influence. There has been praise for the non-verbal and action emphasis theatre of Grotowski in Poland. (And, of course, there are many artistic directors in this country.) Many innovations are changing the whole theatre scene. It is not, however, our purpose to discuss individual directors so much as it is to point out the tools with which the director has to work—to give him the freedom to use all his imagination and originality. We may then judge how he has achieved his effects and evaluate his production and his artistry.

─── WHAT IS THE ACTOR TRYING TO DO?

HOW WELL HAS HE ACCOMPLISHED IT? ───

THE ACTOR'S SUBSTANCE

The role he is playing as set forth by the playwright and as interpreted by the director and the actors

☐ *His tools:* voice, body, diction, mental and emotional powers, personality, talent

THE ACTOR'S FORM

School of acting
Aesthetic style
Period
Play
Character being represented
His approach to his role (may also be considered a part of his technique)

THE ACTOR'S TECHNIQUE

The areas of acting
His personal style
Tests of acting

←─────── WAS IT WORTH THE DOING? ───────→

THE ACTING AND THE ACTORS

THE ACTOR IN ALL OF US

The talented actor must possess the three "I's"
Imagination ~ Intelligence ~ Industry
—Ellen Terry

. . . which properly applied projects the three "V's"
Vitality ~ Variety ~ Validity
—Stanley Kahan

Acting in all its many aspects is one of the most fascinating areas of human behavior. Everyone is to some degree an actor, in more than one sense. The very instant that we *consciously* endeavor to affect the thought or action of another we are acting. The success we have in attaining our goal is the measure of our success as an actor—just as the measure of the performer's success on stage is his effect on the emotions and the thinking of the audience. In this sense the most successful parent, teacher, minister, doctor, lawyer, or salesman is also the most successful actor. It is not our province to consider further this type of acting, although we believe that there is art here, and that, no matter what profession one may plan to follow, valuable lessons may be learned in any well-organized course in the art of acting.

The universal instinct to act must be partially responsible for the fact that almost every individual feels, perhaps secretly, that he could be an actor. This is not true of the other arts. Ask someone to play the piano, paint a picture, design a costume, or build a set, and he will probably answer: "Oh, I couldn't. I have no training. I wouldn't know how to begin." But ask the same individual to take part in a play! There may be momentary hesitation, but there will also be a reaction of pleasure; if someone declines, it will rarely be from a feeling of incompetence. The principal reason for this is that good acting looks so easy and so natural. The finer the performance, the surer the uninitiated are that "All one needs to do is learn the lines and be natural." George Kelly has expressed this universal phenomenon in a one-act comedy entitled *The Flattering Word;* the theme is that to make a friend one need only tell that person that he should have been an actor. George Jean Nathan once said: "Criticism of acting amounts to little more, save on its highest levels, than a reflection of the critic's notion of himself in the actor's role."

From earliest childhood we all find pleasure and escape in any game of "let's pretend." This experience has also been a part of almost every individual's adult life as he has sought the opportunity of getting out of himself, being someone else, living in his imagination, and experiencing emotions and situations often removed from his everyday existence.

To those on the sidelines, the life of the actor is apt to seem to be a round of interesting experiences, public acclaim, applause, curtain calls, easy living, and personal freedom. Actors are always in a position of prominence. They possess a beauty, a charm, and a personality not often found in the mundane lives of the general public. It is little wonder that the actor's life looks fascinating from afar. The truth, however, is not so simple, for the profession is far from an easy one. It involves hard work and serious vocal, physical, and mental training. It demands personal sacrifices, for the theatre is a jealous master. It requires a natural talent and necessitates long hours of study and intense concentration, great imagination, persistence, determination, and, above all, discipline. These requisites are not recognized by those who feel that anyone can act. Historically, acting is one of the most ephemeral aspects of the theatre, but at the moment of its existence it may be the most rewarding. Once concluded, the actor's performance lives only in memory. Thus, with the death of the last individual who witnessed the genius of Edmund Kean or Sarah Bernhardt, the contributions made to man's aesthetic pleasure by these great artists went out of the world forever. It was Edwin Booth who said: "An actor is a sculptor who carves in snow." Nothing vanishes so completely as a stage production.

During and immediately after a performance it is often the work of the actor that commands the greatest attention. It is not unusual for the playwright, technicians, and director to be completely overshadowed by one actor's electrifying performance. History abounds in exciting stories about the great moments on the stage of Kean, Forrest, Booth, Bernhardt, Cooke, Duse, Garrick, Jefferson, Burbage, Siddons, Matthews, the Barrymores, and many others. All these artists had triumphs, heard applause, took bows, read notices, and were heroes of the hour; but the future will find these moments recorded only in the books or in the memories of those who were privileged to witness the performances. We have photographs of the scenery and costumes, and we can read the script, but the work of the actor lives only for the moment. In the twentieth century we have perfected a method of recording the artists' voices and actions. For those who have seen the actual performance, these recordings or pictures can rekindle the flame; but those who have access only to the mechanical reproduction miss the all-important human quality.

Just as good acting is very difficult, so is its evaluation. Critics of the past were not able to agree upon the relative merits of our greatest actors. If experienced critics are divided in their opinions of the work of the giants, then, conceivably, lesser critics will find greater difficulty in agreeing about the art of lesser actors. One need only read the major New York critics the day after an opening to understand that even the most experienced professionals may differ widely in their evaluations of the actor's work. Every player may be mentioned in one or more reviews, but one actor's work may be regarded in one review with high praise, in another given the cursory dismissal of "adequate in the role," and in a third criticized adversely. There are many reasons for this, but one is that acting is based primarily on emotion, and emotions do obstruct the viewer's objectivity.

Perhaps nowhere in the theatre is the element of prejudice more apparent than in the analysis of acting. We like or dislike an actor, although it may be impossible to give any logical reason. These prejudices are often purely psychological in nature. Many of our most popular actors have attained their status not because of talent or imaginative acting, but because their personalities, physical appearance, or charm has caught the imagination of a large segment of the population. Although these individuals—and many could be named—rank high in general esteem, they often lack dramatic talent and owe their success only to the uncritical public acclaim through which they were elevated to prominence.

This is not to be critical of these successful performers, but any evaluation of their work should include an understanding of why they became so popular. It was Henry Irving who said: "What makes a popular actor?—physique. What makes a great actor?—imagination and sensibility."

Another reason behind the difficulties inherent in criticism of actors is the rapid evolution of acting styles. We need only observe a motion picture of a few years back to realize that acting styles change almost as quickly as style in dress. The great actors we read of in history might not seem so magnificent to us today.

Furthermore, an actor's work with a role may change from performance to performance. Such an alteration may be due to physical or mental changes in an individual actor or in other members of the company. It can also stem from the reaction of the audience. Leading actors have stated that their acting varies considerably for matinees (which are attended largely by women), for evening performances early in the week, and for the holiday crowds on weekends.

A featured player who has worked for years with one of our current stars has said that this actor's greatness is never fully realized except by opening-night audiences, either in New York or on the road. The general pattern is the same, and he may never give what could be called a bad performance; but that extra something that lifts and captivates an audience is certain to be present only on opening nights. This is not intentional on the part of the actor; it is just that critics and first-night audiences bring to him an added stimulus. *Variety*, the theatre weekly, does a series of follow-up reviews in which plays that have been running for several months are re-reviewed. Often the acting is reported to be greatly altered from the opening performances—sometimes not as effective, sometimes much improved.

Such alterations in the playing of a role from performance to performance should further point up the futility of arguments about acting, even when the participants have observed the same performance, for in addition to the subjectivity involved, the actor's art is probably less well understood than any other art of the theatre. Standards are confused, principles are misconceived, definitions are often unclear, and technical problems are unfamiliar to the vast majority of any audience. The fault lies in the fact that acting is too often judged according to personal whim rather than by well-defined artistic standards. It is frequently said that "the best acting is the least acting," which is to say that the best acting is so "right" that it seems not to be acting at all. The final answer may lie in the words of a fine old actor, Louis Lytton, who concluded a lecture on the subject by saying: "Acting—after all is said and done—is only a matter of opinion."

It is the purpose of this chapter to formulate a set of definitions, classifications, and principles that will serve us not only in understanding the actor's form and technique, but in establishing a common ground on which to base evaluations. Our first task, then, is to agree on what acting really is.

A DEFINITION

Perhaps the most common simple definition is: "Acting is make-believe"; there are few who would deny that the statement is true as far as it goes. Whether or not an actor really feels his role, both he and the audience are well aware that the experience is feigned, that the actor must consciously control his voice, body, mind, and emotions, and that he must always pretend to be something he is not. But acting is much more than this. If it were make-believe only, we could cite any group of children playing house, cops-and-robbers, or cowboys-and-Indians as perfect actors. The statement does not mention the craft, the technique that must be combined with the make-believe. The actor, in addition to pretending, must memorize and rehearse his lines in order to create a personage who says and does at a specific moment just what the character must do in cooperation with the other actors and in a manner that has been planned by a director. He must be conscious simultaneously of the audience and of its ever-changing and unpredictable reactions, but he must not permit the audience to realize that he is aware of their presence or response.

This awareness can lead to a second popular definition: "Acting is doing consciously on the stage what people do without thinking in everyday life." On the surface this statement too appears sound, for it tells exactly what the actor must *seem* to be doing; it fails as a definition because acting must go much farther than mere imitation. An actor, even in the most realistic or unrealistic theatre, must constantly select, enhance, exaggerate, conventionalize, and project just those aspects of the character and emotion that he wants the audience to grasp. Furthermore, such a definition eliminates all other aesthetic styles, for the characters, language, and situations that have come to us from the Greeks, the Elizabethans, the neo-Classicists, the Restoration, the eighteenth century, and the avant-garde do not picture the reality of here and now. Each of these periods and each playwright of each period paints for us a particular kind of theatricalized reality. The actor must sense and project with truth that special world.

A third definition is: "Acting is the art of abandoning one's own personality, taking on the personality and feelings of another character, and making these assumptions appear real to the audience." It is what some actors do. This definition may partially answer some of the questions we raised about the previous definitions. Critics have praised performances by saying: "He *was* Hamlet (or King Lear or Willy Loman) The characterization was so complete that no evidence of the actor's own voice, gestures, mannerisms, or personality was apparent. He seemed even to grow in stature!" This is high praise, and such an actor certainly must have been convincing. But what of the many stars of screen, television, and stage who always seem to be themselves? What of the actor-personality who draws millions to the box office?

Many further efforts to define acting could be made. For our purpose, however, the most satisfactory definition we have been able to devise is that:

> *Acting is the art of creating the illusion of naturalness and reality in keeping with the type, style, spirit, and purpose of the production, and with the period and the character being represented.*

"Art" implies recognition of form and technique.

"Illusion of naturalness and reality" indicates the all-important aspect of "seeming to be" rather than being.

"In keeping with the type" recognizes that the playing of tragedy, melodrama, comedy, and farce is very different.

"Style" indicates both the aesthetic and individual style of the production, for not all acting is good in the same way or good for the same thing. There is a particular type of acting needed for a play by Somerset Maugham and another style for a play by Neil Simon or Samuel Beckett, just as there is a difference in the way we would play Oedipus, Hamlet, Tartuffe, Oswald Alving, and Willy Loman. There are many kinds of truth and reality other than those expressed by realism. It is these *other* truths that can only be expressed adequately through the right acting style.

"Spirit and purpose" involves the very important aspect of *playing the play* and keeping within the bounds of what the production is trying to say and do. The spirit might be high camp, burlesque, tongue-in-cheek, deadly serious, or just for fun. The purpose or goal might be escape, exaltation, propaganda, or enlightenment.

"Period and character being represented" can set the time and locale. This can be very helpful in further developing truth, consistency, and believability.

To summarize, John Dolman once described good acting as:

> Being neither wholly realistic nor wholly unrealistic. It is sufficiently realistic to be intelligible and suggestive and to arouse the necessary empathy; it is sufficiently consistent to be convincing; and it is sufficiently unreal to preserve aesthetic distance and to leave something to the imagination.*

* John Dolman, Jr., *The Art of Play Production* (New York: Harper & Bros., 1946), p. 227.

THE ACTOR'S SUBSTANCE

The actor, as an artist, finds his substance in the role itself. His chief sources of information are the speeches of the character and what the other characters of the play say about him. Frequently, the playwright has given him some indications in character descriptions. If it is an historical figure, there will be additional sources. Equal to any instructions that can be found in the script are the desires of the director. There must be full agreement between the actor and the director as to the interpretation of the role. This agreement is the framework of the actor's substance.

THE ACTOR'S TOOLS AND THE ELEMENTS
OF DRAMATIC TALENT

The actor as artist is unique, for he *is* his own instrument. His tools are himself, his talent, and his ability to develop both. Unlike artists in some other creative fields, he must work through and with his own body, voice, emotions, appearance, and his own elusive personal quality. All these he uses as a painter uses his paints or a composer his notes. As an interpretative artist he employs his intelligence, his memory of emotion, his experiences, and his knowledge of himself and his fellowmen—but always he is his own instrument. By his form and technique he channels through that instrument the playwright's character and projects it to the audience. As that audience we do an actor great injustice when we do not realize and honestly observe what he has brought to the role—physically, mentally, emotionally, and culturally—as well as what he has done *as an artist* to develop these qualities and then how, as the artist, he has used himself to create and project the character we see. In a very real sense the actor is three separate entities—an *individual,* an *artist,* and the *character* he portrays.

In addition to a normal body, adequate vocal powers, and some mental acumen, any good actor must bring to the theatre a further attribute that we call dramatic talent. Like any other talent, this is a gift from some superior power. He who possesses it should regard it with great pride but be ever conscious that he deserves no credit for its presence. It is a mystic element, a priceless jewel that by some peculiar twist of fate and nature comes with birth and is found in many forms and combinations.

The first and most important acting attribute is *imagination.* Without it one might as well give up the theatre at once, for acting is always an ability to respond to imaginary stimuli. The actor must relive every situation, appreciate and understand the thinking and the emotions of another individual, and express and project this imagined existence to an audience. As an adjunct to this all-important quality, he must possess *sensitivity* and *sensibility*. The first is a thorough awareness of his own feelings and emotions; the second, a thorough consciousness of the feelings and emotions of those around him.

The fourth necessary ingredient in an actor's talent is some *personal quality* that makes him truly distinctive. Helen Hayes once called it "human warmth." It could be a physical characteristic, a mental trait, an emotional response, or some strange combination of these. It means that the individual exists in terms of the theatre; his personality is capable of going vividly over the footlights; he possesses some contagious quality of voice, some great beauty of presence—a fine theatre-mask, a skin that takes make-up, eyes that can be seen, cheekbones that will not crowd them. Perhaps it is a sense of timing, some asset that is peculiarly attractive and theatrical, some personal quality that can infuse his whole intrepretation with a kind of fire that is capable of exciting an audience. Every actor must possess such a gift to some degree, and when it is present in abundance it has given us such names as Duse, Bernhardt, Garrick, Barrymore, Gielgud, Lunt, Fontanne, Olivier, Jefferson, Booth, and Forrest.

The next important item is "stamina." By this we mean health, physical strength, courage, determination, drive, and a willingness to sacrifice. The theatre demands all this of anyone brave enough to join its ranks. The actor must face hard study and dull exercises; he must have the readiness to develop his voice, body, and a command of his intellectual and emotional powers. He must know life and human nature and recognize the total range and value of the mind and spirit. Such training demands the foregoing of personal wishes and hopes and all other ambitions.

To imagination, sensitivity, sensibility, a special quality, and stamina, we must add the "actor's five senses"—a sense of the *mimic*; a *stage* sense; an *audience* sense; a sense of *timing, rhythm,* and *tone*; and a sense of *taste* and *proportion*.

One's imagination is useless unless one can express for others by his mimicry that which his imagination has created for him. The stage and audience senses involve a feeling for, and an "at homeness" on the stage, and an understanding of its particular demands; they involve the ability to sense the pulse of the audience, an inner voice that tells just how long a pause can be held and the split second after a laugh when the next word should come. Coupled with these talents and their training is the sense of timing, rhythm, and tone—the ability to pick up the proper rhythm when the one established in rehearsal has been momentarily broken by an unexpected incident on stage or in the audience. It is an inherent or acquired feeling for the play and its spirit, which can be adjusted to the ever-differing reactions of an audience and to any of the minute human alterations of the established rehearsal pattern. The actor must at every moment be in tune not only with the whole production but also with *this* performance!

Finally, there is the actor's sense of taste and proportion: his ability to evaluate and appreciate the best—to put first things first; to understand values both in and out of the theatre; his realization of what he owes the theatre as an institution personally and artistically.

If talent is inherited, then great actors are born; but good actors, reliable actors, and even successful actors are developed if they, as individuals, possess sufficient desire, ample drive, and an ability to work harder and sacrifice more than in any other professions. Already the reader may be questioning these terms: "great, good, reliable, successful." In our opinion, the difference between a great actor who is successful and a good or reliable actor who is successful is in exact proportion to the presence or absence of the attributes listed above and his development of them. *Talent* he must have brought to the theatre with him; *skill* or *craft* he must have learned.

THE ACTOR'S FORM

SCHOOLS OF ACTING

One frequently gets involved in discussing whether the actor who is completely different from his everyday self on the stage is a greater or lesser actor than the individual who plays a role close to his own age and personality. If we are to be consistent in our criticism, we must start with Goethe's first question and not be concerned with which of these schools is the more difficult or artistic.

What we consider the actor's "school" is determined by whether he elects to go to the role that the playwright has written and make himself over, physically and vocally, to fit that imagined character, or whether he brings the role to himself and makes it over to fit his own natural vocal and physical characteristics. This is not really an overt decision, for it is determined by both the actor's personal talent and the demands of the role. It is easier and more natural for some actors to go to the role and thus become what we call "impersonators." The actors are often referred to as "character actors." We prefer the term "impersonator," believing that *every* role is, in reality, a character role.

Those who bring the roles to themselves we call *interpreters* and *commenters*. The characters they play bear close resemblance to themselves in age and appearance; they interpret the parts without wholly losing their own identities. In our realistic theatre, with its trend to type-casting on both stage and screen, this school is much in prominence. We emphasize, however, that these actors are commenters on the role as well as interpreters of it. This "comment" is of the utmost importance in good acting, and it involves the art of the actor in subtly giving us his own feelings about the character he is playing and all that character is saying or doing. As an artist he not only discovers, interprets, and projects the thoughts and emotions so that they are wholly clear to the audience, but he enhances that interpretation with his own particular talents, understanding, experience, personality, and charm. The character he plays will have taken on new dimensions as it passed through his mind and body to the audience. His voice may retain its natural quality, and he may use the same gestures that we have seen him use in other roles, but there will always be something new and different in the performance that makes this specific character an individual.

There is a third school of acting that gives us what we choose to call the *personality actor*. He is common to all dramatic areas but is more frequently seen in motion pictures and television. These actors have been defined by John Mason Brown as "the suave or tough, the charming or the brusque, the handsome or the portly 'straight' actors whose only, but whose quite considerable, talent is to be their off-stage selves on stage." * They are frequently the most popular and the busiest actors of our day, for as personalities they have attained enviable reputations. Their great box office appeal is due to their appearance, sex appeal, physical or vocal idiosyncrasies, or some special qualities that have strong mass appeal. They are what Mr. Brown further calls "the most delightful and serviceable contributors to our theatre of understatement."

In studying the actor's form it is necessary to determine which school he has chosen to follow. This may be difficult the first time we observe an actor, for we may think that what he brings to us of himself is actually a part of the character. After John Kerr's third Broadway appearance, Eric Bentley wrote:

> When I praised Mr. Kerr in two earlier plays, I though I was praising acting. I now wonder if I was really praising a certain sort of per-

* John Mason Brown, *The Art of Playgoing* (New York: W. W. Norton & Co., 1936) pp. 193–94. (Quoted with the permission of the Estate of John Mason Brown.)

sonality—perhaps only a certain sort of sex appeal emanating from a pouting, indolent, insolent sort of face and a helpless, dead voice. In the next role he undertakes, let Mr. Kerr prove me wrong.*

AESTHETIC STYLE

In our definition of acting we place special stress on the word "style." The actor working in a Greek play will follow the more formal style of acting; in Shakespeare, the romantic style; in a play from the Restoration or eighteenth or even nineteenth century, there will be varying degrees of what may be termed the "declamatory style"; and in a conventional modern play, the more realistic style of acting. Brecht, in his epic theatre, eliminates all naturalism, stylization, and mannerisms, since he believes it is utterly impossible for an actor to relive the life of another. Each absurdist play calls for its particular style.

Shakespeare's admonition is good advice in every age: "Suit the action to the word, the word to the action; with this special observance, that you o'erstep not the modesty of nature, for anything so overdone is from the purpose of playing, whose end, both at the first and now, was and is, to hold as 'twere, the mirror up to nature." The "nature," however, may vary from play to play and certainly from period to period; it is the duty of the actor to conduct himself so that he plays in key with the play as well as with the period and the character that he is representing. Developing this unity of aesthetic acting style in a production is, as we have shown, the work of the director, but the actor's projection of that style is his own domain. On this count a realistic play is, of course, easier, for the actors can find the nature they interpret all around them. They are presenting a world that is familiar to the audience. In any other acting style the performer must use his voice and his body in a much different manner. The bigger voice and gestures coupled with the formality of a classic role or the abandon in gesture and tone of the romantic style will frequently bring the criticism of "over-acting" from the untrained critic. In the declamatory style an audience may come closer to accepting bombast or broad playing and recognize it as part of the play. This style lends itself to the theatricality desired in the avant-garde productions.

As an extension of the aesthetic style there is a production style. This is often referred to as "playing the play," and it involves a unity of intent and projection by all members of the cast. The production style is determined by the director, who may desire to play the script with the utmost seriousness or with a tongue-in-cheek approach. He

* Eric Bentley, *What Is Theatre?* (Boston, Beacon Press, 1956), p. 6.

may wish all his actors to play as actors who are merely telling a story or he may want them to seem actually to become the characters they are portraying. The production style may mean that a farce is played as a comedy or a melodrama as a farce, that a fantasy may be played as if it were actually occurring, or a romantic play done realistically. Production style is found at its best in London, where actors may work together for a long period of time. We are told that it excelled in the older stock companies, where the same actors worked together for years.

The lack of unity of style in a production is one of the most serious weaknesses in our American theatre. It is due to the fact that so few of our actors work long together and under the same director. Only this constant association over a period of time can bring about a thoroughly consistent style. Herein lies one of the great values of a repertory company.

THE ACTOR'S APPROACH TO HIS ROLE

From the very first appearance of an actor down through the succeeding years, there is always a debate as to whether or not an actor really experienced or felt the emotion he portrayed while he was in a certain role. Interesting as such a debate is, an answer is really not pertinent to our discussion. We are interested only in whether or not the *audience* feels, for to move the audience emotionally is the ultimate goal of the actor. This the actor accomplishes by his technique, which is: his means of projecting his art.

With this in mind, we shall do no more than define the two most common approaches to the art and craft of acting.

One approach is referred to as *the method* and springs from the writings of the great Russian actor and director Constantin Stanislavski who, early in this century, recorded his theory of acting. Translation difficulties and the variety of adaptations of his theories have given rise to a great controversy over what he really practiced or meant. Basically he is believed to have endorsed the importance of actually feeling—at least, in having the emotion start within—and the importance of producing only those outward gestures and movements or readings that grow out of that emotion. In short, the actor should work from the inside out and should be possessed by the emotion of the role. The fountainhead of this acting theory is The Actor's Studio in New York and its director, Lee Strasberg.

The opposition to this theory includes those who approach the role from a more objective point of view. Placing a greater emphasis on the craft, they would start from the outside and work in. After examining the role and coming to know the individual, they decide on his walk, his feelings, thoughts, and then consciously *act* or *do* the things they feel he would do. They might be said to follow the old James Langue theory in psychology that said that action preceded emotion—that we run and then become afraid; that we talk rapidly and loudly and become angry.

In the modern theatre these actors are commonly called "technicians," who use the *technical approach*. They act consciously by doing a specific thing for a specific effect. They do not disavow a certain amount of feeling, but they are more interested in control—physical and emotional. They demand discipline and a technique that assures a performance that is consistent performance after performance.

Since the early fifties there have been many new and fascinating concepts to help the actor to perfect his craft. If the reader's interest lies in the area of acting, he should be familiar with theatrical games, improvisations, transformations, etc. All have their followers and each has, undoubtedly, helped many to develop whatever natural talent he may possess. In this book, however, our interest is only in the final result and not in the method of attaining it.

Great acting can and does come from both the method actor and the technical actor, and there are prominent stars who are fervent advocates of each. Our conclusion is that either is acceptable (with the truth lying somewhere in between) just so long as the result gives the audience a consistently moving and convincing performance. If an actor's approach to his job detracts from the performance in any way, if he seems not to be in control of his body, his voice, and his emotions, or if his technique is apparent—the most common criticisms of the two approaches—then the actor has fallen down as an artist.

THE ACTOR'S TECHNIQUE

Acting is both an art and a craft. The *art* of acting can not be taught; it is essentially the talent that an actor brings to the theatre. The *craft* can be taught, for it consists of learning how to train, use, and develop that talent. Helen Hayes once put it very well when she said: "Talent is not for sale, but the best way of packaging and displaying that great gift is!" This packaging is called technique and is frequently referred to as the actor's personal or individual style. Any actor soon learns that feeling and inspiration are not enough. They are only as good as the informed technique that must support them. Stanislavski, in his book *Building a Character*, said: "Without an external form neither your inner characterization nor the spirit of your image will reach the public. The external characterization explains and illustrates and thereby conveys to your spectators the inner pattern of your part." *

The best technique is sensed rather than seen. It enhances natural talent but must never be obvious. An old actor summed it up very well when he said: "Ham acting is when the actor gets caught using his technique."

Margaret Webster, the eminent actress and Shakespearean director, put it in other words when she said:

> When an actor rises to the greatness of his vision with the full armory of his physical powers—that, if his voice be great enough, is genius; and only when his physical prowess outruns the fervor and truth of his vision may he be labeled "ham."
>
> Ham acting is technique in excess of emotion. Keep the two in proportion all the way up, and you will finally arrive at a theatre which is as exciting as it is honest, as theatrical as it is true.

AREAS OF ACTING

Regardless of which school of acting the actor may follow or what style the play demands, there are three specific areas that concern the actor. They are called the "areas of acting":

The technical (physical)

The mental (intellectual)

The emotional (spiritual)

The material of the technical area is similar to the scales one must learn in music. It involves the way an actor gets about the stage— walks, sits, gestures, moves, and handles himself and the props. It includes his breathing, vocal training, and projection. It is the ease and convincingness with which he can *do* all that the audience sees and hears. All these attributes are basic to the actor's work. They can be taught and must be mastered before an actor can be really effective, for he must first be master of himself with his body and voice fully controlled.

The second area concerns the actor's mental approach to the role. He must have analyzed the character from every angle—understood his thoughts, feelings, and actions, his relationship to the play and the other characters. Again, his approach is not of as much importance to us as are the results—whether or not he is able to project a well-

* Constantin Stanislavski, *Building a Character* (New York: Theatre Arts Books, 1949), p. 3.

rounded, honest, and believable character who could actually do and say the things we see and hear.

We have many actors who have very successfully mastered these two areas. In the commercial as well as the noncommercial theatre there are those who never go beyond and who are considered "good actors." They are often referred to as "technicians" and even sometimes rise to stardom, but they rarely attain the status of "great actors."

The third and most vital area of acting is the emotional (spiritual), and it is extremely doubtful that it can be taught. This is the area that Lillian Gish had in mind when she said: "Acting can not be taught—it can only be learned." No one has ever witnessed work in this third area without being conscious of it. The experience may have lasted but an instant, or it may have pervaded a scene or an entire play. It may have been evident in only one actor—but it is a quality that lifts the actor to a higher plane of creation and gives the spectator a special excitement or pleasure. It furnishes those wonderful experiences in the theatre that one carries in the memory forever. Instances of its presence come to us in stories of great actors and their performances. If one has known the experience, the point is clear—if not, further discussion would not help.

Once again we quote John Mason Brown, who has described this third area most effectively:

> Then there are the precious few, standing at the top of their profession, whose high gift it is to act themselves, to adapt their spirits to the spirits of the parts they are playing, to possess and then to be possessed, by the characters they project, and to give them the benefit of their beauty and their intelligence, their sympathy and their virtuosity, their poetry and their inner radiance, their imagination and their glamour.*

TESTS OF THE ACTOR'S ART

Our primary demand of an actor is that he be "professional," and we define that word as does the dictionary: "being engaged in, or worthy of the high standards of a profession—the result of experience and skill in a specialized field." John Gielgud further defined it in an address to the graduating class of the American Academy of Dramatic Art in 1965 by saying: "What is a professional except somebody who is disciplined, skilled, flexible, obedient, punctual, fairly tidy, and who knows how to behave in the theatre."

* John Mason Brown, *The Art of Playgoing* (New York: W. W. Norton & Company, Inc., 1936), pp. 193–94. (Quoted with the permission of the Estate of John Mason Brown.)

Beyond these definitions we shall consider six areas of judgment for the individual actor. Using our imaginary puissance, we should answer these questions after rather than during the performance, for it is in memory that we can better analyze just what it was the actor did or did not do to make us believe him in word and action.

Our six questions are:

1. What does the actor bring to the role in voice, body, and personality and as an individual?
2. Is his acting fresh?
3. Is his acting restrained?
4. Is his acting easy?
5. Is his acting convincing?
6. Does he fit into the production as an integral part of the whole?

1. *What does the actor bring to the role in voice, body, and personality and as an individual?* It may be imagination, a dynamic outgoing personality, temperament, a quality or style that is peculiarly his own, a voice or body that distinguishes him, or an air of authority that makes him master of all he does or is supposed to be. Off the stage he may be completely ordinary, but on the stage he must bring something definite to the role. He must have *authority* and be in full command of his body, voice, emotions, and the whole dramatic situation. The artist should ever be in the ascendancy, guiding and controlling the character. It is evident in the way he handles emergencies, such as a late entrance, a missed cue, an accident on the stage, or an unnecessary disturbance in the audience. It is recognized in the actor's command of what we have already called *stage* and *audience* sense.

How effective is the actor in the use of his *voice* and *body?* Normally the voice must be pleasant in pitch and quality and be capable of adequate variety. The actor must always be heard and understood and speak without strain. His diction (articulation, enunciation, and pronunciation) should be sharp and clear, but must never attract attention to itself. Unless it is a part of his characterization, it must show no evidence of dialect or of a particular section of the country. He should have sufficient command of his vocal powers to impart the nuances that give originality to line readings—for unusual shadings that reveal hidden or new connotations in a line indicate not only a brilliance of conception but a voice highly trained in the art of expression.

The actor's body must be completely coordinated. His movements must be graceful and his gestures used only to reinforce his voice. Every physical action must grow out of the character. Each must be clear, logical, interesting, purposeful, and truthful.

Does he possess an *individual style* that distinguishes him as an actor? No wise actor ever attempts to copy any part of another's style. To imitate does not make the actor a disciple of those he copies, but only a tiresome imitator.

Like any art, acting demands planning, precision, and discipline. The only place for experimentation is rehearsal. What the audience sees must have been worked out in detail.

2. *Is his acting fresh?* Regardless of what the printed program may say, the events on the stage are supposed to be happening now! No matter what period in history is being presented by playwright and actors, we have the right to demand that it give us what William Gillette called "the illusion of the first time." It is most important that each speech, each look, each action carry with it the impression of never having been said or done before.

This "illusion of the first time" should be evident in the manner in which the actor comes into a room, locates an object, reacts to the lines spoken by other members of the company, and it should be felt in the tone of his voice. It can be especially evident in the fleeting expression of the eyes and face that appears just before the actor speaks a line. It is seen in the position of hands and feet and in the attitude of the body. It is of importance not only to the art of the actor, but also to the sustaining of the "half-faith" of the audience. It is the great test of the actor's thoroughness, his honesty, and his sincerity. Each audience has the right to demand this freshness.

Note how the actor sustains his role. Does the character grow and change as the play progresses?

Many times an actor will give all he has during the first act. This can only mean a plateau of monotony during the remainder of the play. He may also drop out of character when he has no lines to speak. The spirit of a musical can be quickly destroyed by the disinterested expressions on the faces of the chorus or of those in minor roles during the song or dance of a featured player.

Much as we have insisted upon technique and important as it is to the actor, few things are more dangerous than technique badly used. Full dependence on technique is common to many actors, particularly after they have played a role for a length of time. Many find it most difficult to recreate the original freshness and sincerity in every performance when they are weary of the role or feel indisposed. This is, nevertheless, the very time that technique can be most valuable when properly used as the outward expression of the correct inward feeling of the character.

The freshness of a performance will suffer on the stage in a way that it can not in motion pictures, for the motion-picture director can take and retake a scene until the actor has given just the desired performance. This is also true, of course, of taped television programs.

3. *Is his acting restrained?* We have said that we go to the theatre to have our emotions touched, that we want the play to happen in us. This comes about more often when the actor shows restraint. He must have power within him, but it must be amply controlled. His job is to stir the imagination of his audience. Tears spilling down the cheeks are usually less dramatic than is an effort at control. The blubbering close-ups that sometimes occur in motion pictures are far less effective than more restraint would have been. The great actor hints at more than he declares. The real power of any line lies in its tone. Watch how the actor builds within a speech or series of speeches—or by pantomime—to a crisis. A crisis need not always be big. Sincere feeling is not necessarily large, but rather deep and honest. The word "ham" is greatly misused in the theatre—most frequently by those who use it to describe something they do not like without quite knowing why. They frequently confuse broad and expressive acting with over-acting. The first we need; the second is bad. We might say that the "ham" expresses small feelings in a big way, while the poor actor expresses big feelings in a small way. Any actor can be insincere, but only an actor with a big voice can be a "ham."

Great acting is more suggesting than actually doing. A good actor never fully portrays the emotion he wants an audience to feel. He builds up to a particular moment, and when that moment arrives the audience takes over and the actor's work is done. The real difference between a great performance and great acting is subtlety. Oftentimes in the theatre—especially in a musical production—a role may call for and receive a bravura performance by a great personality, a performance that is memorable but which lacks the subtlety of great acting. Mae West and Tallulah Bankhead are outstanding examples.

This valuable quality of restraint is evident in the speaking of lines, in the handling of the body, in the grasp and expression of an emotion, and in the smoothness and integration of all these elements. It never permits over-acting or over-stating, but rather relies on suggestion plus imagination and the intelligence of an audience.

4. *Is his acting easy?* The audience must be totally unconscious of any effort. All hard work must have been done before the opening night. In performance the actor must be the master of himself vocally, physically, and emotionally. This is technique at its best. Whatever he does *seems* so natural that it is accepted without question. The perfect performance is one that seems to the spectator so easy and so right that he is tempted to remark that he, without training, could do as well as the artist.

Observe the success of the actor in the "art of doing nothing." It means that he must be a part of the scene even when the playwright has given him nothing to say and little to do. This is one of the actor's most difficult tasks, for acting is not as much acting as reacting. It is these moments that challenge the actor's integrity, sincerity, and imagination. They call for great personal control and restraint. To be successful when given a speech and stage center is not nearly so great an achievement as to be always an important and necessary part of the picture without detracting from it.

Note the actor's sense of timing, his use of pausing, phrasing, and holding. The term "time value" is sometimes given to those moments when words are not spoken but the emotion and mood of the scene flow on. There can be poignant moments when the actor plays upon the imagination of the audience through gestures, suggesting a similar personal experience to the spectator that would have been lost had the actor resorted to words.

There is no single distinction more obvious between trained and untrained actors than in their sense of timing. The inexperienced actor rushes forward, fearful that the audience will think he has forgotten his next line, but the true artist makes the most of every time value, knowing that there is greater power in the suggestion of an emotion than in its actual delineation, that he can often create more in the mind of the audience by the correct pause than by words.

Timing is most important in comedies. Watch how easily the actor plants a laugh, allows it to build to a peak and breaks in with the next word at just the right split-second. In this context, observe closely the actor's sense of rhythm. At its best, the give-and-take between the actor and the audience resembles a tennis game, with the actor creating a perfect rhythm by varying his speeches according to their response.

This sense of timing is of no less importance in the serious play. The actor's command of the pause, his use of the time value, and his feeling for the exact instant for speech or silence are his most precious tools for holding and moving the audience.

5. *Is his acting convincing?* Every item that has thus far been mentioned on the subject of acting contributes in some way to this question. The most devastating criticism of all is that of the spectator who says: "I did not believe it," for the ultimate goal of every actor is to make the audience *believe* him in everything he says and does. His actions must at all times be rightly and fully motivated. His role must be synchronized with the whole production.

Sometimes characters carry such conviction that audiences find it hard to accept them outside the part. Actors have been hissed on the street and refused service in public places while playing the role of a villain or obnoxious character.

Make-up and costuming make their contributions to the actor's world of make-believe. Make-up varies with the lights and auditorium. There is also the problem, especially in the noncommercial theatre, of the young actor or actress playing middle-aged or older roles. The actor should make up for the middle of the house but should strive not to apply make-up too heavily for the front rows. It is better to err with too little than with too much. The professional theatre, with its emphasis on type-casting, has simplified this problem to a great extent, but make-up is still an exceedingly important factor in the actor's believability.

Both professional and nonprofessional presentations are often guilty of allowing their costumes to overpower them. It is most important to wear the costumes of a period play with ease. The Shakespearean ruff and cape, the tunic of the Greek theatre, the ruffles and breeches of the Restoration, the bustles and hoop skirts of the nineteenth century can wreak havoc in a production unless the actors have learned to wear them as skillfully as they have memorized their roles.

In a production of a Civil War play presented by a summer theatre company in the East, the mood was completely destroyed when a young lady arose from the sofa and turned too quickly in her walk to the upstage door. The front of the hoop caught on the corner of the sofa and the rear of the hoop caught her on the back of the neck. The warm weather had caused her to reduce her undergarments to a pair of red shorts, and the audience suddenly had thrust before its eyes something that looked like nothing so much as the Japanese flag.

6. *Does he fit into the production as an integral part of the whole?* Note how he gives a scene that does not belong to him as well as how he takes the scene that does. It is not always to an actor's credit to say that he stole the show. Many times he may have been playing to the audience in a bid for popularity. Actors have been known to cough, drop handerkerchiefs, and use a variety of other means to attract the attention of the audience when the best interest of the play demanded that attention be given to some other player.

Sometimes the star in a commercial production is guilty of upstaging the other members of the cast. The same error may be committed by noncommercial players who have no intention of stealing the scene, although they, too, have been known to do it deliberately. Part of the theatregoers' work is to study each actor and understand his importance in the scene. Only then can we decide whether he is the selfish actor who wants to stand out from the others or the cooperative one who is interested only in making his contribution to the production as a whole.

If we do not consider all of the above we are denying the actor as an artist and we are robbing him of his profession.

THE MOTION PICTURE AND TELEVISION ACTOR

Although the names of actors are used to attract an audience into the motion-picture theatre, the intelligent theatregoer will realize that the actors themselves often contribute less to motion pictures than would appear on the surface. Unlike the stage, in films the major contribution is often made by the director and the technicians.

Whereas the theatre calls for the art of collective acting, motion pictures permit the art of individual acting. Not often is there need for much group work. (We are excepting, of course, the many familiar mob scenes.) When an individual or small group becomes important, the camera moves in, and we have the close-up. This eliminates all but those few involved. This is not possible on the stage.

The motion-picture actor is often incidental to the background, while in the theatre he must always be superior to it. It is not unusual for the inanimate object to be equally, if not more, effective than the actor. A close-up of a crushed hat or flower or a broken glass can express stark tragedy. The camera can pan down on the turning of a doorknob and produce near panic in the audience. The impossibility of this on the stage is obvious. Herein lies a very important facet of motion-picture art that we should recognize and appreciate when it is done well. Sergei Eisenstein, the famous Russian director, has called it:

> The process of arranging images and feelings in the mind of the spectator . . . A broken ladder, a woman weeping, and a grave. . . . these can tell a complete story and create an emotional response.

In the theatre the equivalent effect could have been attained only through much dialogue and acting. Unless we are aware of this great assistance given the actors by the imaginative work of the director and technicians in the development and the projection of emotion, we shall have bypassed one of the principal elements of motion-picture art. We must have emotion—but we must not confuse it with acting.

The motion-picture actor must work without any audience reaction, but he has as many chances as he may need to "get it right." The stage actor, on the other hand, inspired by the audience's response, has but a single opportunity in each performance. This does assure the assembled motion-picture audience that it will see only the finest performance of which the actor is capable. On the stage there is always the possibility of human error, e.g., failing memory, a misplaced prop, accidents of any kind. These deviations bring with them new sets of circumstances to be faced by the actor and an increased interest and element of surprise or enjoyment on the part of the audience. The tests for freshness and ease are not as valid in the cinema, for the two-dimensional photographs we observe may have been made months or even years ago. They are crystallized and changeless. In making those photographs the artists had many opportunities to get the exact effect they wished. We see only the result. As Rouben Mamoulian has aptly said, the audience watches the "future become the past" in a stage production and the "past becoming the present" in a motion picture.

From the actor's viewpoint there are further factors of differentiation. The stage actor must sustain a role over a long period of time, but he does have the opportunity to build an emotion logically from its very beginning through its crisis. On the screen few scenes last more than two minutes and more often are a matter of seconds in length, and they are not taken in sequence. The motion-picture actor need not sustain his character except for a very short time, but he must be able to catch any degree of emotion without having the opportunity to develop it from the beginning. He must start each scene cold.

The stage actor must project to the very back row, both vocally and physically. The microphones and cameras solve this problem in the pictures, but the mental concentration must be far more perfect. The very proximity of the camera means that a single extraneous thought passing through the actor's mind during a close-up may register in his eyes or in some minute facial expression. Such details would be unseen by even the front row in the theatre. On the screen the actor must project and enlarge his gestures and facial expressions on the long shots and show great restraint on the close-ups. On large motion-picture screens an eyebrow may be many feet in length, and the least quiver can destroy a complete mood. The actor must constantly adjust his work to the camera. It follows then, that our tests for restraint and believability might be equally valuable in either medium.

Actors on both stage and screen have found it possible to be successful in the other medium, but the techniques of each require study and concentration, both by them and by those of us who sit in the audience.

In the realm of television, the stage and screen actors have each found their backgrounds to be both an advantage and a disadvantage. The extensive use of the close-up has been advantageous to the screen actor who was accustomed to it. The stage actor, able to project to the back row of the balcony, vocally and physically, has found a need for adjusting to these new circumstances. On the other hand, the stage actor trained to the arena style of production finds that experience most valuable in the area of television acting; the stage actor can memorize a role and sustain a character throughout a long scene—he possesses greater consistency in his control of body, voice, and imagination, in contrast to the motion-picture actor, who has always played very short sequences and had the opportunity of repeating scenes time after time until the exact effect was attained. The cinema actor has been accustomed to numerous mechanical devices, such as countless lights, numerous microphones, props, and the ever-present camera. The stage actor must adjust to being the servant of all this mechanical equipment and to being fenced in by it.

Both are faced with using a far smaller playing area and the necessity for following exact movement, turns, and angle directions as well as a most limited rehearsal period. The months usually given a motion picture and the weeks for rehearsing a stage production have shrunk to a matter of hours for the television drama. Television actors are conscious of these and many other details even while they work to develop a characterization; remember the lines, the exact direction, the idea of the play, and the relationship to all the actors; keep one eye on the director, and remember that their audience is really the cameraman—even should there be a studio audience present. Yet they dare not permit the discerning eye of the camera to show any of the frustrations that these technical elements can bring about. Add to all this the constant pressure of the clock ticking away the seconds, the vagaries of the sponsors, advertising agencies, and public ratings, and we can see why television acting is perhaps the most demanding of all.

It is important to understand the problems of the television actor, but we should not allow them to enter into our final evaluation of his work. They are merely occupational hazards.

In television actors are far more the victims of type-casting than in either stage or cinema. Both the difficulty of and time required to change make-up and the risk involved of its being detected by the camera have almost eliminated the opportunity for actors to play characters unlike themselves in age or general appearance.

And now we would consider some of the special talents required in this difficult field. Even more than on the stage, the voice on a microphone must have a pleasing quality, a wide range, good articulation, and a diction that does not attract attention to itself—unless it is essential to a particular characterization. It should also possess a style of its own and show rich feeling and intelligence. Through the voice and, visually, through the actor's body we get the sense of a speech, the purpose or intention of the character. There is no room for generalities in the reading of a line on television; the *specific* must always be in evidence. The actor must be especially careful of his word groupings, his emphasis and pauses. Variety is a vital factor. It is as if he were speaking to us personally, for he is physically so close to us and our attention is so concentrated on him and him alone.

Characterization is of central importance. Because of the extreme proximity, this can be at once easier and more difficult. A greater control of facial expression and eyes, in fact the whole body, is essential. The slightest movement can be made meaningful or merely distracting. The close-up eliminates the possibility of any momentary relaxing that might be possible on the stage. A character in the theatre exists, primarily, in the imagination of the actor. By that actor's selection of physical and vocal externals he transfers that character to the imagination of the audience. He must know exactly what lies behind each speech if it is to be properly motivated. In any realistic characterization the television actor has greater opportunity and more details with which to work—but with that opportunity he also has more responsibilities and a need for greater control.

The motives of the characters are the source of all action and reaction in theatre presentation; as viewers we are always interested in them. On the stage our chief interest is on the speaker and his actions. Both in motion pictures and on television we frequently see more of the reactions of characters being acted upon. One can detect in any television program the great emphasis the cameraman, director, and even playwright place on reactions by focusing the camera on the face and action of the person being spoken to. This is an aid to both playwright and actor, for it pushes the story forward by telling the audience two stories at once. We are able to look inside the character's mind and to hear his thoughts.

Thus far we have considered only the straight dramatic programs, those that might fall easily into one of the four accepted types— tragedy, melodrama, comedy and farce. The last three, as in both the other media, are much in the majority, especially melodrama and farce. Farce, which in television is often referred to as "situation comedy," is one of the most popular types. Here we find the same star appearing week after week in an only slightly different situation. More often than not the leading roles are all played by the same actors. Within the program each character may have a name, but rarely do we remember or use them. The series is known by the name of the star and depends solely upon his or her personality as a showman. Here the word "performance," as Mr. Atkinson has distinguished it from "acting," comes into even better use, for these programs are to television what the comic strip is to the newspaper. Characterizations are based on such simple and single traits as being extremely shy, very bold, most stingy, in search of a husband (or wife), unusually quarrelsome, meaning well but always doing the wrong thing, or just being an "average family."

A companion to this "situation comedy" is found in a long series of morning and afternoon programs. The only difference lies in their melodramatic and pseudo-serious situations.

In each case the script, week after week, is practically the same—the situations varying just a bit from the previous episodes. We do not condemn these cartoons *per se*. They may serve some purpose but must be recognized for what they are. Individually we may or may not care for the personality that is being presented, for the character he portrays, or for his particular acting style, but as critics we must view them objectively.

In this discussion we have considered some of the added problems of television acting and its variations as compared to the stage and cinema. What has been said should not alter our final decision about the artist's effectiveness as an actor, for the six tests of the actor's work are just as valid for the motion-picture and television actor as they are for the stage actor.

THE TECHNICIANS' SUBSTANCE

The mood, story, idea, or theme of the play
The purpose of the play as conceived by the playwright
and as interpreted by the director and portrayed by the
actors

□ *Their tools:* line, mass, color, wood, materials, paint,
jewelry, cloth, accessories, leather, light, shade, sound,
camera

THE TECHNICIANS' FORM

The aesthetic style or period of the play
The way this style is being expressed
The point of view of the whole production

THE TECHNICIANS' TECHNIQUE

How the artist has chosen to express the form by his
own interpretation
The use of color, design, personal style in area
The effects created by all technicians through color
Personal style in interpretation
Distribution of light
Camera angles, and so on

────── WAS IT WORTH THE DOING?──────

THE BACKGROUND AND THE TECHNICIANS

WHO ARE THE TECHNICIANS?: THEIR TOOLS~THEIR SUBSTANCE

In our present-day theatre we have come to take for granted the elaborate and detailed scenery, the appropriate costumes, and the lighting that not only affords excellent visibility but contributes so much to the mood of the production. One does not often realize that these embellishments are all comparatively new, and that for hundreds of years the script and the actors were considered to be the only real essentials in the theatre.

The scenic background can be traced to a hut that stood at the rear of the Greek playing area. This small building was used by the actors to make the changes necessary to impersonate other characters. Its basic purpose was *concealment*. When this structure was enlarged and decorated, especially by the Romans, the second purpose of scenery came into existence: *decoration*. During the Middle Ages, when the theatre existed primarily in the Catholic Church, the various stations of the church served as stages, and the third element of *mood* came into the picture. With the coming of perspective in the art of painting a fourth purpose was born—that of *suggesting* the locale of the action. Only within the last one hundred to one hundred and fifty years, and in our own realistic theatre, has the effort to *portray* place been a factor.

Historically the scenic background has come to us in the above order. There are those who feel that it is also the order of importance so far as its artistry is concerned.

Until the theatre moved inside in the Middle Ages the only lighting was furnished by the sun. Once indoors, candles were used for illumination, sometimes altered by the placing of colored silks or wine bottles in front of the flame for a special effect. The first real control of quantity in illumination came with the discovery of gas in the mid-nineteenth century. Any real artistry in stage lighting is as new as our modern electricity and our ability to control its quantity, color, and distribution. The electrician is the youngest artist in the theatre. He and his lighting equipment have been the greatest single influence of the twentieth century on theatre production.

The third technician is the costume designer; efforts to costume actors in the proper period and dress for the character being portrayed have been evident for only about two hundred years.

A fourth technician is often considered to be the musician, though his contributions have varied in prominence from the Greeks to the present day. He is responsible for the musical background and his work is frequently worthy of special consideration and study. In our present discussion we have included the work of the composer only when a special score has been provided, with the technician in charge of all sound in the production. So far as the live theatre is concerned these are the technicians: scene designer, lighting designer, costume designer, and musical composer and/or sound man. Musical comedies, operas, and revues also need the choreographer, the artist in charge of the musical arrangement, the lyricist, and others.

In motion-picture or television production we find all the technicians listed for live theatre, and in addition the very important cameraman. He is the artist responsible for using most effectively those techniques that particularly distinguish motion pictures and television from the stage. He must possess a knowledge of all the technical resources and special means involved in the "shooting" processes of cinema or TV.

The substance of all these technicians is the same, namely, the projection of the story, theme, mood, or idea that the playwright has conceived within the particular interpretation given to it by the director. Each works with his own tools, whether they be line, mass, color, wood, paint, cloth, leather, jewelry, accessories, light, shade, sound, or the camera with all its possibilities.

With his individual tools each technician has certain obligations to carry out if he is to give the maximum assistance to the playwright, the actors, and the director in projecting the substance of the production. His form involves the use of his tools (or materials) in portraying the aesthetic style or period in which he speaks, his means of projection, and even the budget with which he works. His technique is how he uses these tools through the form that has been established, and, at the same time, speaks as an individual artist. It is how he expresses himself through his personal style or design in the medium of his creation, be it scenery, lighting, costumes, sound, or camera work.

THE SCENE DESIGNER

The scene designer and the director must come to a clear understanding of the type, style, mood, spirit, and goal of the total production, for the setting has one primary purpose: to help the actor. The only time an audience should be conscious of the scenery—as scenery—is when it is first seen, either on entering the theatre or when the curtain rises. Therefore, the first requirement of all scenery is to be functional and, in the words of Raymond Sovey, the distinguished scene designer, "to furnish the production with a satisfactory *locale* in mood and spirit." Mr. Sovey always preferred the word "locale" to "scenery."

When he designed the locale for *Our Town* in 1938, Sovey made it the most effective background for that script. It was a startling innovation, but Sovey was an advocate of the "atmosphere theory" and an associate and disciple of Robert Edmond Jones. He was determined to create a world that was absolutely *right* for what was to be said and done in Thornton Wilder's imagined world. The simplicity, truth, and universality of the script was reflected in the sparse background and props of the production. Sovey's locale became so much a part of the imagined world that it has been copied in almost every production of the play around the world. For those familiar with any one of the more than two hundred "locales" that Raymond Sovey created for Broadway production, his recognition of "truth" rather than realism is immediately evident.

When *Our Town* first opened there was great fear among the advocates of scenery—especially realistic scenery—that a trend might develop toward its elimination. A cartoon appeared in *The New Yorker* in which two of Helen Hokinson's characters were seen at the box office inquiring: "Is this a play with or without scenery?" Sovey once said: "The real question should be—is there any theatre in the scenery?" We should always ask ourselves: how theatrical, how helpful, how provocative, how meaningful, or how detrimental is the atmosphere that has been created by the scenery?

One of the most serious arguments against a realistic set is that it can detract from the actor and the play by weakening illusion in challenging comparison, and thus that it interferes with both empathy and aesthetic distance. Since the early fifties, thanks to both the epic and the absurd influences, the realistic setting has been on a steady decline, except when absolutely essential. Few settings will ever fit solely into a single classification, for freedom permits borrowing from any source that will contribute to the total effectiveness of the artist's goal in creating the proper locale. He does what he feels should be done, and after the set is completed, it is the audience who labels it. It is this labeling that presents one of our greatest problems in discussing scenery, and the difficulty lies in terminology. Unfortunately, few authorities are in full agreement about the exact meaning of all the words they use to describe the settings in our modern theatre.

For our purpose we shall consider the six most commonly accepted scenic styles to be realism, simplified realism, impressionism, expressionism, theatricalism, and formalism. The first four lean toward the imitation of life and, in theory, propose to help the actor develop and project the mood and spirit of the play. The latter two tend to "suggest" rather than "portray," serving only as a satisfactory background and, in theory, help the actor by staying out of his way. Our interpretation of each style will be presented in an effort to show how that style makes use of line, mass, and color.

REALISM

The ultra-realistic set is an effort to portray place consistently, convincingly, and as completely as possible. There was a period when naturalism—which can only be defined as extreme realism—would have come first, but it is rarely seen today. In the realistic set great attention is given to small detail, and every effort is used to give evidence of reality. David Belasco even imported the authentic furniture of Madame du Barry to set the stage of the play about her life. At other times he insisted upon running water, a stove that actually prepared the food on stage, and such realism as knocking radiators. The sunsets that he contrived through lighting are still praised for their naturalistic beauty by those who saw them in the theatre more than half a century ago.

Such duplication of life and such lack of suggestion was and is sure to call forth criticism from among those who accept the premise that all art is selection rather than representation or that the theatre must *seem* real and not *be* real.

SIMPLIFIED REALISM

This is an effort to use the advantages of realism, but to simplify them so that the setting may meet more accepted aesthetic standards. In the simplified setting no effort is made to fool the audience. If some detail is unconvincing, it is eliminated. Some evidence of unreality may appear, which is not a distraction but an admission that the setting is only an illusion of reality. The goal of the artist is a suggestion of the exact locale rather than a representation of it.

IMPRESSIONISM

This style gives only the impression of locale and carries simplification even further. It is what Jo Mielziner calls "implied scenery" and is more concerned with mood than with detail or any effort to do more than merely suggest place. It demands more imagination on the part of the audience. Because the element of exaggeration is almost inevitable, most impressionistic sets take on some form of stylization. An impressionistic set normally uses only partial walls and set pieces, often silhouetted against a plain cyclorama. Doors, windows, and lesser details may only be indicated. This style of scenery is very effective for staging classical plays—in fact almost any style of drama except the ultra-realistic.

EXPRESSIONISM

This is the most difficult of all to describe, for it borrows from all the other arts by using music, rhythm, line, mass, color, and light. The designer distorts the lines of the scenery to express the mental or emotional distortion of one or more of the characters. Plastic forms, levels, and sharp angles are used most frequently. It has found great favor with the avant-garde. Whereas impressionism appeals principally to emotion, expressionism appeals more to the intellect. It is often seen today in combination with other styles.

THEATRICALISM

This is both the oldest and the newest style and also the most versatile, for it lends itself to almost any production style. Until the realistic theatre came into existence it was the accepted practice. This was especially true after the development of perspective in scene painting. It reached its height during the nineteenth century, when wings and backdrops were frank admissions of unreality, even though they attempted to suggest the locale with their painted exteriors or interiors, including minute details. A theatrical set today presents scenery as scenery. It may be decorated—attractive and in the mood—but it makes no pretense of being more than scenery. There is no attempt at any illusion of reality. It is only background and not environment. Actors act in front of it rather than in it. The theatrical set is most frequently found in musical comedies and revues, although the avant-garde theatre also finds it of great value.

FORMALISM

Formalism makes use of the natural background that belongs to the building, the theatre, or the auditorium where the play is being given. It employs neither representation nor suggestion. Perfect examples are simple draperies, the pulpit of a church, or an outdoor stage. Such a set is ideal for poetic tragedy. It was the only stage or setting used by the Greeks in their outdoor theatres or by Shakespeare in the Globe Theatre. Background is only background and not expected to be considered scenery. Formal backgrounds are very effective for the classics or in modern unrealistic plays suited to presentational or audience-centered production.

In the following illustrations Don Swanagan, New York designer, has envisioned a realistic setting and then imagined how that same setting might appear if the generalizations concerning realism, simplified realism, impressionism, expressionism, and theatricalism were carried out. Formalism does not appear, because that style uses the natural locale and, therefore, has no scenery.

STYLIZATION ~ SYMBOLISM ~ SPACE STAGING

There are three contributing factors that may be used in conjunction with any one of the six scenic styles listed above. They are stylization, symbolism, and space staging. In the confusion of terminology the most abused word of all is "stylization." In this book we will think of it primarily as an adjective modifying one of the major styles.

Stylization works with and depends upon the imagination of the audience. It appeals to the emotion or to the intellect as the scene designer may desire. It involves chiefly exaggeration of some kind, a special treatment of an established scenic style.

The scene designer may stylize according to the *period* of the play or the *mood* of the play. The first might involve designing a near replica of the old Globe Theatre stage for the production of a Shakespearean play. In Shakespeare's day this would have been a formal setting, but now it would be *stylized formalism.* An equally imaginative designer might conceive a series of backdrops and wings to represent the various settings in *Ten Nights in a Barroom* as it was done in 1890. This could be *stylized theatricalism.* In his approach to *Androcles and the Lion,* for

Realism

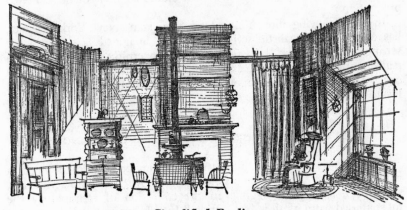

Simplified Realism

example, another artist could paint an imaginative, blown-up, water-color forest scene, depicting the wildest sort of trees and flowers, to suggest the tongue-in-cheek fantasy expressed by Bernard Shaw. This has been termed *artistic child's play*, for such a design would give the artist's impression of the play's mood and could be called *stylized impressionism*. The word *stylized* should thus always be used as a modifier and in association with one of our modern scenic styles.

Symbolism involves the use of some object that through its association will establish the thought, locale, or mood. The imagination of the audience will then fill in the remainder of the setting. Such symbols may be used as a judge's bench for a courtroom, a blackboard for a

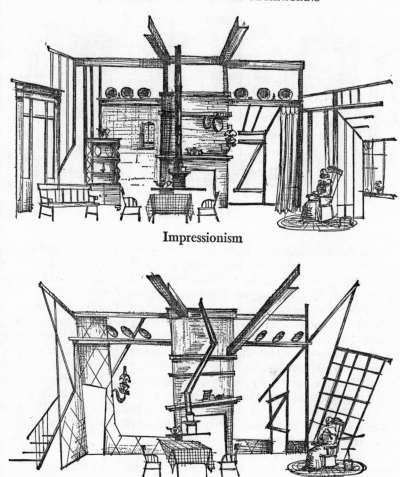

Impressionism

Expressionism

schoolroom, a figure of the Virgin Mary for a religious mood. Further objects of symbolism might be a flag, a church window, a jail door, and so forth. Concrete symbols may become *symbolic impressionism.* Abstract motifs of a similar nature may thus create a *symbolic expressionism. Our Town* could be said basically to have used a formalistic background, but when the church window was projected on the back wall, and the soda fountain was implied by the use of two chairs and a plank, and the ladders suggested stairways, the scene designer was using a *symbolic formalism.*

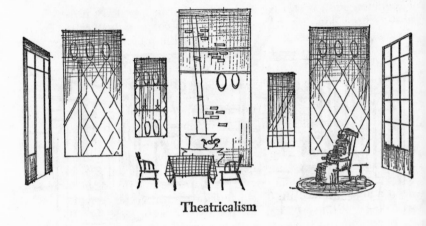

Theatricalism

The third contributing factor is called *space staging*, if the director possesses sufficient lighting equipment and a satisfactory cyclorama—preferably black velours—he can do some remarkably artistic and imaginative work. Space staging involves a dark stage with a spot light picking out of the void the characters and scene involved. The lighted area may indicate anywhere or everywhere. Space staging is usually found most practical and effective when a drama calls for a great many short scenes or when it is necessary for the action to move from one locale to another very rapidly. As much or as little as the designer may wish in the way of props and scenery may be used to indicate locale. When, through space staging, an effort is made to suggest an exact place, with the use of skeleton scenery and props, the scenery is referred to as a *simultaneous setting*, and more often than not is impressionistic in style. Any number of locales may be found on the stage—a country store, the pulpit of a church, a bedroom, an office—all adequately equipped to give a definite impression of place. Each can be brought into focus merely by concentrating the light on that particular area. A second and somewhat simpler effect is known as *multiple setting*. The principle is the same except that there is no effort to suggest exact locale, and the stage may be practically bare of scenery and props. It follows more nearly the staging in an Elizabethan theatre, with its outer and inner stage, balconies, and so on. Like it, the script is depended upon to indicate locale if that information is necessary. With multiple staging little more than light and characterization are used. Space staging can be used effectively in many plays but is less suitable in those that attempt realistic representation.

We emphasize that styles in scenic design are constantly changing and that audiences should no longer expect standard sets, but instead look for imagination and artistry on the part of the scene designer.

Experimentation is exciting and audiences can encourage it. Much has already been done by the educational and community theatres in this direction, and the scenic contributions of the professional theatre have shown marked progress in the past decade.

With this explanation of modern scenic trends, the chart on the following page may help to summarize and further clarify the goals and means of the scenic artist in our theatre today.

These six modern trends in scenic art, plus the three contributing factors and combinations of any or all, are a very important part of the scene designer's form. His technique (personal style) is the way he has expressed the central idea or mood of the play through the aesthetic style in his use of mass, line, color, levels, and stage decoration or decor. To appreciate the technique of any artist one must constantly ask *how* he has accomplished his result and how creative he has been in his work—how it differs from what might have been done.

The motion pictures are rarely concerned with the subject of scenery as we have been discussing it. Their surface realism demands the real thing, although the "real things" must be selected and arranged and the selection may be detrimental as is often evident when the living quarters of the characters in a motion picture are not in keeping with their economic status or position in society. The background sometimes seems to attract attention to itself by its beauty or by some unusual quality. Rarely do the motion pictures try to use any but the realistic setting—even when the substance would seem to suggest some other aesthetic style. Television, on the other hand, has been more creative in this sense. As a result TV gives us examples of some of the styles we have already discussed. The result has proved to be both imaginative and artistic.

THE LIGHTING DESIGNER

It is necessary that the lights and scenery work in complete harmony, for one is most dependent on the other in the total effect, and both are there only to help the actor tell the story.

The lighting designer knows that the stage must at all times be sufficiently lighted to permit visibility without strain, but, as in all art, this visibility implies selection. The upper corners and walls should not be as brightly lighted as are the areas where the action of the play takes place. Good lighting must select and emphasize that aspect of the production that needs pointing up at any given moment. A doorway, for instance, need not be lighted during an entire scene, but it must be sufficiently illuminated when an important character makes his entrance

PURPOSE OR GOAL	MODERN SCENIC STYLES	CONTRIBUTING FACTORS
	Realism (Naturalism) consistent convincing complete	*Stylization* Exaggeration to suggest period or mood
Helps actor to portray mood— spirit— emotion by assisting him	*Simplified Realism* no effort at completeness; unconvincing details eliminated	*Symbolism* One object represents another— or a great deal more
	Impressionism less detail—only essentials to suggest locale and emotion	*Space Staging* A light picks a scene out of a void and illuminates a portion of a multiple or simultaneous setting, which may suggest or represent a specific or a generalized locale—anywhere or everywhere
	Expressionism still suggests, but by distortion; tries to portray feeling in physical set	
Helps actor by staying out of his way	*Theatricalism* Background decorated and used as background only	
	Formalism Building or surroundings as they are	

if the needs of the play demand it, though the audience must not be aware of this change in the illumination. Artistic lighting should accentuate the proper emotional and psychological qualities of the play. Through the use of quantity, distribution, and color the electrician paints the stage with light—much as a painter does his canvas—and in so doing creates a mood of mystery, impending disaster, warmth, frigidity, time of day, season of the year, or almost anything else.

In supplying adequate visibility, selecting proper emphasis, and creating a mood or atmosphere, the designer may work realistically or theatrically. This is his form or style. Realistic lighting represents nature and must have a natural source, such as a window with its sunlight, a lamp, or a fireplace. These areas must be in brighter light than other parts of the room, for the lighting must follow the laws of nature. Light, as seen through a window, must alter with the time of day or year, but that alteration must be imperceptible at the time it is made.

For those plays that are lighted theatrically it is not necessary to consider the light source. Needless to say, such plays are the joy of the artist-electrician, for his imagination is the limit just so long as the lighting does not overpower the production itself. The theatrical use of lights is possible in the production of almost any style other than the realistic.

It is equally important in realistic lighting, where illusion is the goal, to eliminate such distracting elements as a spill of light on the proscenium, teaser, or tormenter or a light leak from back-stage. A poorly illuminated room, supposedly just off-stage and into which characters are to pass, can quickly destroy this illusion. An audience can be greatly disturbed by a flickering lamp or the reflection of some light in a mirror or picture. Extreme care must be given to the light outside windows and when the impression of distance or sky is required. Where illusion is not important, as in a Brecht play or much of the avant-garde, there is no limitation on the electrician's use of lights. Instruments are exposed; lighting is rampant and may often be remembered as a most important facet of the whole production. The avant-garde has made great use of theatrical lighting and often in a highly imaginative manner.

In our theatre, the lighting designer is an artist and each of his effects is the result of careful planning and of his knowledge of human emotions, the specific needs of the script, the flexibility and limitations of his instruments, and his own creative imagination.

The lighting designer in motion pictures or television has essentially the same obligations, though his contribution is often confused with that of the cameraman, for they must work together in perfect harmony. While the stage electrician, working with the director and scene designer, lights the stage for his actors and the audience, the motion-picture electrician lights for the director and cameraman, who, in turn, translate the story for the audience. Here it is the camera that sees, for on the screen the camera is really the eyes of the audience.

THE COSTUME DESIGNER

In any dramatic production today we have come to demand that the costumes fit the period, the season, the locality, time of day, occasion, and mood of the scene. They must have the correct line and color to do the most for the character projection and for the individual actor playing the role. Each costume should be stageworthy in that the lines and design are sufficiently exaggerated to carry over to the audience and that the costume is so designed that it can be worn with ease.

The costumer's form is again determined by the aesthetic style and historical period of the play's action. Certain eras are known for specific characteristics in dress, such as the midline decoration of the Egyptians, the chin ruffs of the Elizabethans, the immaculate collars and cuffs of the Puritans, the hoop skirts of the Civil War, the bustles and leg-of-mutton sleeves of the late nineteenth century, and so on. The artistic costumer takes these constant elements as dictated by form and simplifies or exaggerates as his artistic nature and the demands of the play may prescribe. This is his contribution as an artist. He must realize the vast range of color meanings and their psychological effects on an audience. He must be conscious of the possibilities in various color combinations as well as the effect of light on pigment. Color must be considered with an eye to harmony, unity, and contrast. (For example, conflicting dramatic forces may wear opposing colors.) Whatever technique is used, it must, above all, be done subtly. The good costumer knows that the actor must stand out against the set but that no actor, unless for a special purpose, must wear a costume or accessory that clashes with the set. In life we may not consider the color of the hostess's draperies or walls in our choice of a tie or dress, but on the stage background must be taken into consideration.

The actor's personality must be given special thought, both as it is in reality and as it is to be in the play, for clothes are as personal as any other aspect of a character. Not only must they be agreeable to the temperament of the wearer, but they must fit the part he is playing. The Chinese Yin and Yang theory, applicable to both men and women, is of interest. The Yin is the sweet, quiet, sensitive, introverted individual, and the Yang, the forceful, strident, confident, forward extrovert. The first seem to lean toward those qualities that we class as "feminine" and the latter toward those we consider "masculine." This theory further suggests that the proper dress for each personality should emphasize his own type: ruffles or softer hues for the Yin; tailored or more positive colors, with an emphasis on the dark, for the Yang. At the same time, exaggeration should be avoided since it has a comedy value, although in some instances this might be exactly what is needed to portray the extremely masculine man or woman, or the extremely feminine. The same femininity or masculinity could be lessened, given its proper status, or perhaps even eliminated by costumes proper in both color and design.

As an audience we must consider both the costumer's originality in creation and execution and his projection of the dramatic significance each costume possesses.

THE MUSIC COMPOSER AND/OR THE SOUND MAN

In our discussion of melodrama we pointed out that the very term implies "drama with music." Even before the coming of melodrama, however, the theatre frequently incorporated some form of music into the production. With the coming of motion pictures a full musical background became increasingly important until today more than 90 percent of our pictures have complete musical scores. Television adopted the technique, and the theme song of many a series has become synonymous with the name of the program and oftentimes with that of an individual performer. The living stage has borrowed from the other media, and original musical scores have become an important part of many modern plays, especially those of a more serious nature. In any discussion of the technicians we must, then, give some careful attention to the artistry of whatever musical background may be present; we must consider both the composer and those who interpret or perform his work.

Until recently music or sound was never intended to stand out in itself, but in some avant-garde productions it has become the most important item through its very loudness. The use of mixed media, with live and recorded sound and music (along with film and slides) has become a fad. The appeal is always sensual rather than intellectual and has gone beyond even the technical demands of Brecht's epic drama and the torture chambers of Artaud. Such extremes are sure to fall out of favor just as soon as the audio-visual machinery and the explosion of electronic and mechanical devices have lost their novelty.

Sound, when used correctly, can develop the mood, build the crises, set the period, and sometimes establish the basic rhythm of production. That it has been raised to an art in itself is proved by the fact that we may not notice the music as such during the performance but will praise it when heard as a separate recording. The use of a familiar tune may sometimes prove a distraction, either by our very recognition of it or because of its association with some personal experience. A further distraction results when in a very realistic sequence the music is not adequately motivated.

Music at its best serves not as a mere substitute for dialogue but as an emotional adjunct to periods of pantomime. Many times this lack of dialogue is not even noticed. To realize the preponderance of music or sound and scarcity of speech in a motion picture, one need but listen without watching for some length of time. The musical score, however, must always supplement and never supplant the acting. The less it is observed, the finer the artistry of the composer. In addition to music, the theatre has utilized sound effects more consciously in recent years. Authenticity is the keynote and perfect reproduction has become a necessity.

Only those sounds with dramatic value are utilized on the stage and in motion pictures, but in the latter the element of sound takes on a different dimension. As an example, we cite the condemned prisoner in the death cell. To him the ticking of a clock takes on a very distinct meaning, which the sound man is able to give the audience just as the prisoner hears it. On the stage this dramatic value would be lost. One can readily see the tremendous empathic possibilities that lie within the province of an imaginative sound man.

His contribution is even more important in terms of the proper adjustment of the equipment as it relates to the musical score, the dialogue, or the combination of the two. His sound equipment may be his form, but the effective use of that equipment and the authenticity of the sound itself are the result of his technique.

THE CAMERAMAN

Motion-pictures are the offspring of the marriage of art and science. It is obvious that the very birth was dependent upon the camera and the science of photography. Never for a moment must we allow this one essential difference between stage and screen to escape us. In essence, the substances and forms of stage, motion pictures, and television are not greatly different. It is in the area of technique that the media differ, for technique is the basis of cinema production.

The two basic elements of the stage are performance and audience. The screen presents a third—often more important than either of the others—the *camera*. Motion pictures are possible without a story, without scenery, even without actors, but never without the camera. That eye guides the audience to just what it wants them to see and interprets that material for them. In this sense, it is both the creator and the spectator, for it determines not only what we may see but how we may see it. In its development the contributions of light and sound and their coordination have lifted motion-picture production to an art in itself. This medium has unquestionably produced aesthetic achievements that would have been impossible in any other form of expression.

The *cameraman*, then, must receive our unbiased consideration as a motion-picture technician. He can build a dramatic sequence without the use of actors, solely through photographic images. It is possible for him to create an intimacy by means of the close-up, with its naturalness in both voice and facial expression. This is an advantage denied us on the stage, where the consideration of projection to the back row is so important. Medium and long shots can either add to or detract from the total effectiveness, and the cameraman's use of them is a part of his technique. Color and light and their shadings are all within his province. Their psychological effect can be tremendous. At times the whole art of motion pictures and television comes closer to painting than to the stage. These distinctions we must recognize and appreciate.

There are occasions when we find ourselves praising the photography more than any other part of the picture. This is wrong if we are to follow our principle that the theatre is a synthesis of the arts. We must learn to appreciate the photographer's techniques and his ability to use his camera. We should understand the "cut," which is an abrupt shift from one angle or distance to another, and the "fade" which acts as does a curtain in a stage production to separate one scene from the next or denote the end of a sequence. We should appreciate his use of the "dissolve" to connect one scene with the following one and yet to show the passage of time. We must also be conscious of the emotional strength inherent in the "montage," that rapid sequence of pictures that can help build to a crisis. We should appreciate the kinds of shots and their variety, the angles, and their total effect on the dramatic significance of the film. We should recognize his art, but only as it contributes to the total effect of the picture as conceived by the director's creation and ultimate authority.

Filmed or taped television shows, with their greater freedom, come closer to the cinema technically—the difference being only that they cannot be as effective in presenting the panorama, long shots, huge crowds, beautiful settings, and the chase. It is true that some television pictures have tried to incorporate these techniques, but the small screen makes them very difficult. This liability is often apparent when we see a regular motion picture—prepared for that medium—being used for television.

Because of the time limitations of the program and the size of the screen, the television cameraman's responsibility is even greater than the cinematographer's. He is second only to the director, and in some programs there is a camera director as well as a floor director who is responsible for the staging and acting. The two must constantly work together. If, as critics, we fail to catch the full impact of the camera as playwright, actor, and technician, we have failed to comprehend much of the cameraman's art.

As a playwright the camera serves as narrator, capable of prowling about the set and among the characters looking at everything. The smallest gesture, action, or prop can become the most important facet of the entire story. The camera can act in a most *objective* manner—as a third person whose purpose it is to show the audience just what it wants them to see, yet never become a part of the action. It can interpret the story, choosing just which character will at any given moment contribute most to the central idea, and giving that character just the degree of importance it wishes. The camera can, in some situations (in a ballet, for example), take on the attributes of another participant and move about among the performers as an integral part of the scene. This is called *subjective* camera technique.

As a technician the cameraman must have a keen sense of composition and dramatic values, a sensitivity for feelings, and a knowledge of psychology as well as art. He must know that too much movement of the camera can have the effect of making the audience dizzy, whereas too little will lead to monotony. There is only a very short time—twenty to thirty seconds—during which the viewer can look at a single picture without losing interest. The cameraman must know just how much of the subject should be included in the picture for the best pictorial and dramatic effect—full body, from the knees, waist, chest, or just the face and head. He must make the choice of angle—side, front, back, or below or above the subject. Psychologically and photogenically, as well as dramatically, this angle can mean much to the artistic or dramatic value. A low camera angle can increase the size and importance of a character, both physically and psychologically; a high camera angle can diminish his importance in relation to the whole picture.

There is more to choosing an angle, however, than merely a desire to do so. Each angle must have a meaning. A shot taken from high above the heads of two lovers in an embrace or from below could only confuse the viewer unless it was an effort to use the camera subjectively and give the impression that someone was observing the scene either through a transom or from a position of hiding. The cameraman must appreciate which view of the face is most pleasing, for individuals are often more photogenic from one side than another. He must be especially careful of the extreme close-up, especially with a woman who may be playing a role that calls for a younger appearance than her own natural one. Few persons can afford to fill the screen with just face and head. The slightest complexion blemish, scar, mole, or perspiration can prove a serious distraction. Costumes can be very attractive from one angle and quite ordinary or uncomplimentary from another. The cameraman must be sure that all pictures are adequately framed on the three sides—especially giving characters head room—which means ample room between the top of the head and the top of the picture. To cut a picture at the hair line of an actor or the ankles of a ballet dancer is a serious error. The cameraman must also choose the movement the camera will make—whether it will move forward or backward, to the right or left, vertically or horizontally. All his work must be without effort. All camera changes must be smoothly done and in complete rhythm with the action and movement of the story. As with other artists we must never be conscious of his technique at the time.

There are other technicians in motion pictures and television—the make-up man, art director, editor, set decorator, special effects man, and so on. The long list of credits that comes at the close of any program gives some indication of what a tremendously cooperative art each of these media is, and we would not belittle the work of any technician. Each must make his contribution to the sum total, the unified effect. If his work is a part of, and never apart from, that single impression—then it is as it should be. If the scenery, the decor, the lighting, the costumes, the make-up, the sound, or the props attract attention to themselves as such, then they are in error, for we should never be conscious of a technician's work while the production is in progress. To notice the scenic design consciously, to be suddenly aware of the lighting, the costuming, the work of the photographer, or the sound is a distraction from the purpose of the play. The work of each must be so "right" that it fits into the general background and is accepted in the spirit, style, and meaning of the production. Only in retrospect do we really appreciate the greatest artistry of a technician. That we are not aware of it—at the time—is the finest compliment he can be paid.

Important as the creativity, skill, and artistry of each technician may be, their complete cooperation with the director and their acceptance of his authority must always be recognized.

RECAPITULATION AND RETROSPECT

RECAPITULATION

In discussions of a dramatic event, many arguments arise because people are speaking about different aspects of the production without knowing it. It is essential that the intelligent playgoer know the following categories and the terms associated with each. All have been presented and explained on the preceding pages. They are listed here as a review and for ready reference.

The seven fine arts are: dance, music, literature, architecture, painting, drawing, sculpture, and—if an eighth is added—theatre or dramatic art. We prefer to consider theatre as a synthesis of all the other arts, the only common meeting ground.

The elements of any fine art are: substance, form, and technique. (The latter is sometimes considered part of the artist's personal style.)

The theatre production as a synthesis of the arts includes: the play and the playwright; the director and the directing; the actor and the acting; the background and the technicians; the audience and its reaction.

The elements of any written drama—as listed by Aristotle—include: the plot or story, characters, thought or theme, dialogue, atmosphere or mood, and spectacle.

The major types of drama are: tragedy, melodrama, drama, comedy, and farce. These types can be combined.

The major aesthetic styles in drama or theatre production are: classicism, romanticism, neoclassicism, realism, naturalism, fantasy, expressionism, symbolism, epic, surrealism, theatricalism, and absurdism. (We prefer to think of "theatricalism" and "fantasy" as styles that can be combined with any of the others, especially when the drama becomes a play.)

The structure of a drama must involve an emotional situation that may possess any or all of the following: exposition, inciting moment, rising action, turning point, falling action, climax, conclusion, crisis, change, conflict, discovery, dramatic action, surprise, and suspense.

The nature of a drama or theatre production can be: journalistic, theatrical, literary, moral, immoral, conventional, avant-garde, propagandistic, social, thesis-presenting, or problem-presenting.

The actor may be considered as three different personalities: individual, artist, and the character he portrays.

The schools of acting produce the following types: the impersonator, the interpreter or commenter, the personality.

The actor's approach to his role can be: based on feeling, working from the inside, often called "the method"; or based on technique (and the James Langue theory of action preceding emotion), working from the outside, usually called "technical."

The areas of acting are: the mental or intellectual, the physical or technical, the emotional or spiritual.

The actor-audience relationship can be said to be: representational or presentational and the intent illusionistic or nonillusionistic.

The spirit of a drama or theatre production may be: an illusion of reality, theatrical (sometimes to the point of "total-theatre"), completely sincere, kidded, burlesqued, tongue-in-cheek, campy, stylized as to period or to mood, artistic child's play, etc.

The purpose or goal of a drama or theatre production is always communication and entertainment; in addition it may be: escape, enlightenment, exaltation, excitement, or amusement, and so forth.

The pillars of the fine arts involve: the originality, truth, imagination, and sincerity of the artist's conception and the unity, emphasis, rhythm, balance, proportion, harmony, and grace of its realization.

RETROSPECT

With the basic assumption that the word "theatre" includes, for our purposes, cinema and television as well as the living stage, this book has set out to outline and explain one theory of theatre understanding and judgment. The concepts and principles on which this theatrical approach is based have been used in an effort to set up at least a temporary criterion for the beginner in his attempt to reach an understanding of why he has or has not enjoyed a given stage, motion-picture, or television experience. Opinions and principles have been presented as such, with the full realization that any playgoer with further experience and reading may modify or even discard much of what he has found on these pages. This is inevitable—the point being that *in so doing he will have set up his own standards of judgment*. This is the first goal of *Understanding Today's Theatre*.

It is said that Shakespeare followed a cycle of first stating what he was going to say, then saying it, and finally pointing out that it had been said. Whether or not this generalization can be substantiated, the purpose of this chapter is to complete this same cycle, examining this book in retrospect as a whole.

We have from the beginning conceived of the fine arts as existing primarily for the purpose of aesthetic pleasure. The theatre has been considered as a synthesis of the arts, because it is composed of all their elements and may therefore be called the meeting ground of the arts. We have supposed that it belongs to the people and that the audience goes to the theatre primarily to have its emotions touched. We have concluded that audiences are different from the individuals of which they are composed, and that accordingly the art of the playwright is the most difficult of all literary work. We have insisted that each artist be ever aware of the fact that the theatre must *entertain* its audience in the fullest meaning of that term, that all entertainment is not art but that all art is entertainment, and that there is something wrong with the art that does not entertain. In addition to its entertaining, the theatre must communicate, and in its capacity as a teacher, challenge the audience in its thinking, improve its taste, increase its knowledge of life and art, and clarify its thinking. In so doing it will thus *create a better audience, which will in turn demand better theatre*. This is the second major goal of the book.

All this must be done while the spectators are being entertained, for the theatre has the right to expect only involuntary attention, the attention that comes without effort on the part of the audience. As an art it is the obligation of the theatre to give the audience more than it could have lived through in the same period; it must suggest life rather than imitate it; and it should *seem* real rather than *be* real. This is accomplished through theatrical reality, commonly called "theatricalism," which we define as "exaggeration under control" and which is found in every phase of the production. This bigger-than-life quality must never cease to be believed by the audience as long as it is in the theatre.

The vast importance of the audience, its reactions, and its contributions to the production must never be forgotten by any of the theatre's artists or those who consider themselves critics. The theatre is in one sense similar to a five-ring circus, with each ring contributing an essential part of the whole production. The five areas are the audience and its reaction, the play and the playwright, the director and the directing, the actor and the acting, and the technicians and the background.

Poetry can be as vital and as alive in the twentieth century as at any time in the past; it has only changed its appearance and may be found in the unity, emphasis, rhythm, proportion, balance, harmony, and grace that each artist can bring to the well-coordinated production. We have accepted the belief that all art is selection, and that it consists of substance, form, and technique. We have defined technique as the artist's means of accomplishing his end. It is the measure of his own creative ability to bring together the substance and the form. We have tried to explain some of the accepted theatre forms and to point up some of the most obvious techniques of each artist. The artist works not only in the hope of sharing his own aesthetic experience with the audience, but of receiving its approbation for his efforts.

We have emphasized that if the theatre is to grow, it must be in a constant state of change and that—at this moment—we are faced with an especially strong and far-reaching revolution that has divided the theatre into two camps—the conventional and the avant-garde. Each has its own very different goals. We have tried to examine these objectives as impartially as possible and to leave any decisions as to their relative values to you—the reader and the audience. Our terminology, for the sake of clarity, has borrowed more from the conventional than the avant-garde, but always we have considered art to be life as seen through the personality of the artist as he creates, interprets, portrays, or suggests some segment of life.

Fully conscious that the three media—stage, motion pictures, and television—can never be compared exactly one with the other, the fact remains that they work with much the same material, employ practically the same artists, and strive for common goals. Therefore, we may evaluate the total effectiveness of each by much the same general standards that we have presented as the ten commandments of dramatic criticism.

Every individual is moved emotionally or aesthetically, depending upon the stimulus, his personal background, and his experience. Unanimity of opinion is neither expected nor desirable.

This book was planned in the hope that it might make the reader understand and demand more of the theatre. It is further hoped that through the influence of these pages he might be enabled to view the theatre with a greater degree of "imaginary puissance," and never fail to take into consideration Goethe's three significant and valid principles for evaluating any work of art. Such an approach demands that our dramatic criticism exist on three levels—the *literary*, which emphasizes the written drama; the *theatrical*, which stresses the creation of beauty through sheer theatre magic; and the level of pure *escape* or amusement, commonly referred to as "show business." Such an approach will allow each artist the freedom to create and will also encourage a *fairer and more honest evaluation of his work*.

If, then, this book has (1) helped the playgoer create his own standards of dramatic criticism, (2) helped him to provide a fairer judgment of the artists' work, and (3) laid a foundation for the building of better audiences who will eventually demand better theatre, a contribution will have been made in the realm of dramatic understanding, discrimination, and theatre appreciation.

Glossary of Theatre Terms

Most of the following terms are frequently used in discussions involving the stage, motion pictures, or television. A knowledge of their meaning is essential. Generally, those that were defined or discussed in the text have not been included here.

ABSTRACT SET. Drapes, single units of doors or windows arranged for music or ballet numbers. No effort at realism or locale. Common in television.

ACTORS' EQUITY ASSOCIATION. Union of professional legitimate theatre actors, with headquarters in New York City.

AD LIB. Generally, words and gestures that are neither written in the script nor rehearsed, but that are improvised by the actor.

A.F.T.R.A. American Federation of Television and Radio Artists. Union for television and radio actors, with offices in New York City and Los Angeles.

ANGEL. Individual who furnishes financial backing for a production, but whose name rarely appears in connection with it.

A.N.T.A. American National Theatre and Academy. Congressionally chartered organization for serving the theatre in all its branches. Supplies advice and various services. Offices in New York City.

ANNIE OAKLEY. A pass or complimentary ticket to the theatre, so called because of the habit of punching holes in such a ticket in the pre-rubber-stamp days.

ANTAGONIST. The character most in opposition to main character (PROTAGONIST) of the play.

APRON. Space on stage in front of main curtain; very wide in Restoration and eighteenth century. Much of the play took place here.

ARENA STAGE. A form of center staging with audience on three or four sides. (See THEATRE-IN-THE-ROUND and PENTHOUSE THEATRE.)

ARRAS SETTING. Half circle of neutral draperies that serve as formal background for the stage. (See CYCLORAMA.)

ARTISTIC FAILURE. Play that may have artistic qualities but that has received poor notices and is a failure at the box office.

ASIDE. Words spoken by the actor in a lower tone. The audience, but not the other characters of the play, is supposed to hear them.

AUDIO. Sound portion of a television show.

BACKDROP. Large flat surface at rear of stage, painted to suggest locale and used with WINGS in seventeenth, eighteenth, and nineteenth centuries. In present-day theatre usually represents sky. (*See* SKYDROP.)

BACKING. A series of FLATS or DROPS placed behind doors and windows to mask backstage area.

BACKSTAGE. The entire area behind the PROSCENIUM arch, but normally during the action of the play the area that is not seen by the audience.

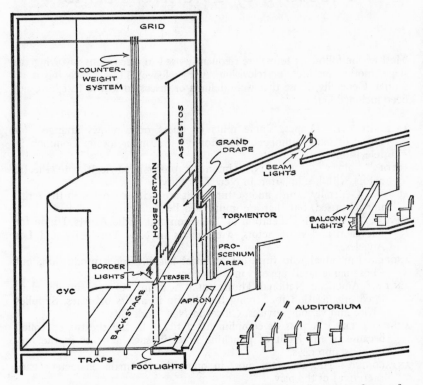

BIT PART. Very small role (described by one actor as "two speeches and a spit"), such as "The carriage awaits, milady."

BLOOPER. Error by some member of cast or crew. Sometimes called "goof" or "boo-boo."

BORDER. A short curtain hung above the stage to mask the FLIES when a ceiling piece is not being used.

BORDERLIGHTS. A series of lights above and at front of stage to light the acting area with general illumination.

BOX SET. Traditional setting with back wall, two side walls, and usually a ceiling to represent the interior of a room.

BROAD COMEDY. Slapstick bordering on farce or BURLESQUE. Overdone for the sake of GROUNDLINGS and lacking subtlety.

BRIDGE. A transition from one scene to another. In radio it is usually music; on television the use of a small object such as a letter, picture, or fan to allow change from one set to the other by an actor.

BURLESQUE. An exaggeration in character traits, stage business, or movement, so overdone that the sense of reality or its illusion is destroyed. Emphasizes humor.

CHEAT. To turn the body to play toward the audience while appearing to be in conversation with other players on the stage.

CLAMBAKE. A poorly constructed or rehearsed program that is much below standard.

CLAQUE. A group in the audience (friends or especially hired) who applaud or react vocally to give the impression of great enthusiasm for the performance.

COMMEDIA DELL' ARTE. A pantomime or drama without any set literary form. The theatre of common people in Europe, beginning with the fifteenth century. It gave us such characters as Harlequin, Pierrot, Columbine, etc.

CONVENTION. An idea, not necessarily true, that the public accepts, for example: blue light for moonlight and yellow light for sunlight (although in reality daylight is more blue). Something that has come to be a part of a style or form.

CONVENTIONAL THEATRE. The accepted theatre building with raised stage, scenery, lights, and PROSCENIUM, with auditorium and audience out front.

CRISIS. Two forces in direct conflict come to a breaking point—one side must give. A series of crises lead to a climax, which is the biggest of the crises and usually the final one.

CRITIC'S CIRCLE. A group composed of all first-line New York critics for newspapers and magazines, who by secret ballot award prizes to the best American and foreign play and musical each spring.

CROSS-FADE. *Audio*—to fade out one sound and fade another in. *Video*—to fade out one picture and fade another in.

CUE. The final words, business, or movement of one character before another begins his own.

CUT. *Stage*—to delete a line or omit certain business. *Screen*—transition from one shot to another.

CYCLORAMA ("CYC"). Curtain or canvas usually hung in a half-circle to cover the back and sides of stage. May represent the blue of the sky or be a plain drape setting. (*See* ARRAS SETTING.)

DECOR. Furnishings, PROPS, draperies, and decorations of setting. (*See* IN-SCENIERUNG.)

DENOUEMENT. The moment when the last suspense is eliminated. From the

French—a literal translation is "untying of the knot." Usually comes with or after the climax and before the conclusion.

"DEUS EX MACHINA" ("a god from a machine"). When Fate (or the author) intercedes to save the action from its logical conclusion.

DISCOVERY. Sudden knowledge—the audience or the character realizes something about himself or another person or a given situation that might alter the whole course of action.

DISSOLVE. The second shot appears on the screen under the first and becomes increasingly distinct as the first disappears. Serves to connect scenes on the screen.

DOWNSTAGE. The part of the stage nearest the audience.

DRAMATIC ACTION. Term used to describe the action that takes place within the play—Oedipus' search for the slayer of Laius, Hamlet's search to discover if the ghost has spoken the truth and then his efforts to right the wrong. What happens in the play to the characters beyond mere physical action.

DRAMATIC TIME. The period that elapses in the action of a script. (*See* PHYSICAL TIME.)

DRESSING THE HOUSE. Scattering the audience by leaving pairs of seats or more empty to give impression of a larger attendance.

DROP. The name given the curtains that are hung from the FLIES.

DRY-RUN. Full rehearsal without the use of cameras.

EMMY. Annual award for excellence in all phases of television. (From "Immy"—an engineering term relating to the Image Orthicon Camera Tube.)

FADE-IN AND FADE-OUT. The light intensity of the first camera shot falls to zero and the second rises to normal value. Serves to distinguish between scenes.

FILM CLIP. Film inserted into a live telecast.

FILTER. An audio effect used to give a metallic quality to the voice, such as when talking over the telephone.

FLAT. A piece of scenery composed of muslin, canvas, or linen stretched over a wooden frame. Used for walls or the backing of a set.

FLIES. The whole area above stage back of the PROSCENIUM where BORDERS, DROPS, and small pieces of scenery are hung.

FLOOR PLAN. A bird's-eye view of the stage, with walls, entrances, and furniture all shown in their proper places.

FLUFFED LINE. A stammer, stutter, twisting of words, or other faulty delivery by the actor.

FLY. To raise scenery above the floor of the stage by use of ropes, battens, etc.

FLY CATCHING. Movement, business, or sound made by an actor to attract attention to himself when emphasis should be elsewhere.

FORESTAGE. The part of the stage nearest the audience when an inner PROSCENIUM is used. Sometimes used interchangeably with APRON.

FORMAT. Style of make-up of a television script. Also used to describe the method or pattern of opening and closing the program. Usually followed from week to week.

47 WORKSHOP. A playwriting course originally at Harvard and later at Yale under George Pierce Baker. It gave us many leading playwrights of the twentieth century.

FOURTH WALL. Technique used in realistic and naturalistic theatre that is completely representational, treating the proscenium opening as the fourth wall of a room, ignoring the presence of an audience.

FREEZE. To stand completely still as if for a picture.

GEORGE SPELVIN. Name often used by an actor for the second or lesser role he is playing within the same play. Sometimes credited to William Gillette, William Collier, Sr., or William Seymour, but generally accepted to have been used for the first time in 1907 in Winchell Smith–Frederic Thompson's play, *Brewster's Millions*. An actor chose the name for a second role. The critics praised "George Spelvin" for his work and the play was a hit. Smith always insisted on listing the same name on future programs, for luck.

GHOST WALKS. A phrase used by actors to denote payday.

GIMMICK. A device or trick used for a special effect, usually in an effort to get a laugh although it may seek any emotion.

GOOD THEATRE. A quality that makes a play especially effective when presented before an audience.

GRAND DRAPE. A curtain above the stage and at the top of the PROSCENIUM arch; it hangs in front of the main curtain, decorates the top of the stage, and reduces the height of the opening.

GRIDIRON (GRID). Framework of wood or steel above the stage. Used to support and fly scenery.

GROUND CLOTH. Waterproof canvas covering usually used to cover the entire stage floor.

GROUNDLINGS. Term used by Shakespeare to indicate the uneducated and untrained theatregoers who sat in the pit and were highly entertained by broad comedy.

GROUND ROW. Profile at the back of stage representing trees, shrubbery, hills, etc. Masks the meeting of stage floor and CYCLORAMA.

HAM ACTING. An exaggerated and insincere performance, notable for noise rather than honest feeling or sincerity. Extravagant gestures, choking sounds, and trickery are used for themselves alone. Should not be confused with BROAD ACTING or PROJECTION.

HAPPENING. A skit or improvised drama built around current world events or personal problems. Diverse elements may be organized into a semblance of structure; frequently nonverbal, with music and sounds substituted for language. Often not subject to logic.

HOKUM. Deliberate simulation of emotion by artificial means, and also the means used. Sure-fire but time-worn theatrical tricks.

HOUSE SEATS. Seats retained by the management to cover errors or to be given to distinguished guests. Released just before curtain time.

IDIOT-SHEET. Copy, cue lines, or other material written in large letters for television actors, announcers, and others.

IMAGE. Picture appearing on the television screen.

IMPROVISATION. In recent times, used as part of some stage productions; popular in supperclubs. More common as an approach to the actor's training. Playing a scene or situation without a script and with both words and action created extemporaneously.

INGENUE. The actress who plays the role of an innocent young woman.

INNER STAGE. In Elizabethan theatre, the small area upstage and enclosed by curtains. It localized action, which moved forward to the outer stage after the scene was underway.

"INSCENIERUNG." German term to describe the whole visual stage picture, including lighting. (*See* DECOR.)

JUVENILE. Young actor; male counterpart of ingenue.

LIGHT LEAK. Light that can be seen through a crack or opening in the set.

LIGHT SPILL. Light that strikes the PROSCENIUM or set and thus "spills over" in a distracting manner, rather than striking just the area it is supposed to cover.

LIVE. Actually present in studio, as opposed to filmed or recorded.

LOCK. Term describing those elements that prevent a character from escaping the results of the conflict.

MASK. To cover from view of the audience with some type of scenery.

MONTAGE. A rapid series of different shots that build to a climax and in doing so give a single impression.

MOSCOW ART THEATRE. Established by Constantin Stanislavski in the last decade of the nineteenth century and until the Stalin regime considered one of the finest theatres in the world.

MUFF. To mispronounce or transpose words or syllables.

MUSICAL COMEDY. A light story, with spoken dialogue interspersed with music and dances.

OBLIGATORY SCENE. The scene of the play which the playwright has led us to expect and without which the audience would be disappointed. Sometimes referred to as "*scène-à-faire*."

OSCAR. Annual award by the Motion Picture Academy for outstanding achievements in all phases of the cinema. (Named after Oscar Pierce, twentieth-century American wheat and fruit grower.)

OUTER STAGE. Forestage of Elizabethan theatre, used especially for soliloquies and most dramatic scenes. Historically preceded the APRON.

PAN. To criticize adversely. *Screen*—The slow rotation of a camera on its axis to show a panoramic view—large or small, horizontal or vertical.

PAPER. Complimentary tickets given out free or at reduced rates to bring in a larger audience. Sometimes called "papering the house."

PENTHOUSE THEATRE. Name given to the first ARENA theatre of this century when it opened at the University of Washington.

PERIPETEIA (PERIPETY). A reversal of circumstances that leads to a result contrary to our expectation.

178

PHYSICAL TIME. The actual minute length of the production, as opposed to the DRAMATIC TIME.

PLANT. Apparently casual insertion of an idea, character, or prop to be used more significantly later in the play.

PLASTIC SCENERY. Scenery built in three dimensions rather than painted on a flat surface.

"THE POETICS." Written by Aristotle (360–322 B.C.). The earliest critical treatise extant dealing with dramatic practice and theory.

POINT OF ATTACK. That arbitrary point where the writer has chosen to begin his script.

PRACTICAL. Scenery that is usable; a door or window that will open, etc.

PREMIERE. First public performance of an art work.

PRODUCER. In America the individual or group who raises the money or underwrites the production financially. In England usually considered to be the director as well.

PROJECT (PROJECTION). *Stage*—To increase size of voice, movement, and gesture so it can be seen and heard in the rear of the auditorium. It "theatricalizes nature," so to speak, by increasing the feeling, but all is done with sincerity. Sometimes called "playing broadly," but not to be confused with HAM ACTING. *Screen*—Throwing the picture on the screen.

PROPS (PROPERTIES). Any articles or pieces of furniture used by the actors.

PROSCENIUM. The wall that separates the audience from the BACKSTAGE.

PROSCENIUM ARCH. The opening in the PROSCENIUM through which the audience sees the stage; the picture frame.

PROTAGONIST. The leading character in the play—the one in whom the audience is most interested.

PULITZER PRIZE. Award given each year to the best play on an American theme.

RAKE. To place the set on a slant. Usually applied to side walls.

REPERTOIRE (REPERTORY). A list of dramas, operas, parts, etc., which a company or person has rehearsed and is prepared to perform. They are sometimes alternated in performance.

REPERTORY COMPANY. Theatrical group that has and performs a REPERTOIRE.

RESOLUTION. The solution of all conflicts presented in the play.

RETURN. A FLAT used at extreme right and left of stage and running off stage behind the TORMENTOR. Sometimes it serves as the TORMENTOR.

REVUE. A series of unrelated songs, skits, and dances, very loosely tied together by the title—usually some topical subject. All pretense of plot is abandoned.

SCENARIO. General description of action for a proposed motion picture.

SCÈNE-À-FAIRE. (*See* OBLIGATORY SCENE.)

SCHMALTZ. Overly sentimental material, usually with music in the background. Sometimes applied to overacting or production.

SCREEN ACTORS GUILD. Union of motion-picture actors.

179

SCRIPT. The written drama from which the play is built.

SET PIECES. Scenery that will stand without support. Used especially in non-realistic productions.

SHOW BUSINESS. Name applied to theatre productions pandering to a non-discerning audience and emphasizing escape or box-office appeal rather than literary or theatrical merit.

SKELETON SETTING. Rudiments of a setting, appealing largely to the imagination of the audience.

SKENE. A small hut in the Greek theatre, used for concealment during a change of costume. It has given us the English word "scene."

SKIT. A short scene of dialogue or pantomime, usually in a satirical or humorous vein.

SKYDROP. A DROP painted blue to represent sky and to mask the rear of the stage; hangs from the FLIES. (*See* CYCLORAMA.)

SNEAK. To bring in music, sound, or voices at extremely low volume.

SNOW. White spots or interference in a television picture.

SOLILOQUY. A speech delivered by the actor when alone on the stage. There are two types: *Constructive*—to explain the plot to the audience, as in many of Shakespeare's prologues. *Reflective*—to show personal thought or emotion, as in *Hamlet*.

STAGE RIGHT AND LEFT. The right and left sides of the stage from the actor's point of view.

STATIC PLAY. One in which very little happens and the characters and situations are essentially the same at the end as in the beginning.

STEAL. Getting from one part of the stage to another without being noticed. Also applied to taking a scene that really belongs to another.

STING. To punctuate with a sudden musical phrase, shout, or some other emphatic sound.

STOCK (STOCK COMPANY). A resident company presenting a series of plays, each for a limited run, but not repeated after that engagement.

SUPERIMPOSE. The images of two shots seen together, one on top of the other. A double-exposure.

TAG. Final line of play.

TEASER. BORDER just upstage and back of the front curtain. Masks the FLIES and determines the height of the PROSCENIUM opening during the performance.

THEATRE GUILD. Producing organization in New York. It works on a subscription series there and in many other large cities.

THEATRE-IN-THE-ROUND. (*See* ARENA STAGE.)

THE THÉÂTRE LIBRE (Paris). Free theatre in France in 1887. Headed by André Antoine, it introduced naturalism and freedom from the artificiality of the nineteenth century.

"THE METHOD." The name applied to the Stanislavski approach to acting; very subjective, introspective, and individualistic.

TONY. Annual award for outstanding work in writing, acting, and design in the New York theatre. (Named in honor of the late Antoinette Perry, American actress and director.)

TORMENTORS. FLATS at the extreme down right and left of the stage near the PROSCENIUM and masking the backstage area. (*See* RETURN.)

TRANSFORMATION. A kind of improvisation used as an acting exercise— sudden breaks and momentary changes by the actor as he goes from one character or emotion to a very different one. No continuity; strives to create great variety in mood and character.

TRAP. An opening in the stage floor, permitting entrances or exits from under the floor.

TURKEY. A dramatic production that has utterly failed.

TWOFER. A coupon that gives two tickets for the price of one. Issued toward the end of a play's run.

TYPE-CASTING. Casting people of the same age, appearance, size, or nature as the character in the play. Mostly an outgrowth of the realistic theatre.

UNIT SETTING. Pieces of scenery—FLATS, pillars, doors, pylons, arches, etc. —that can be put together in various combinations to furnish different settings.

UPSTAGE. Toward the back of the stage. For many years the stage was higher in the back and slanted down toward the footlights and audience. This is still true in some European theatres.

VICTORIAN. Applied to the era of Queen Victoria or the second half of the nineteenth century in England. Noted for prudery and ostentation in art.

VIDEO. The sight portion of a television program.

WASHINGTON SQUARE PLAYERS. An amateur group that grew into the present successful THEATRE GUILD.

WELL-MADE PLAY. A name given those plays written in mid-nineteenth century which followed a set pattern or formula in their construction. Now has a derogatory meaning.

WINGS. Off-stage space to left and right. Sometimes refers to wing pieces used in series of two or three on either side of the stage as part of the wing and backdrop set.

WIPE. The first camera shot is peeled off, revealing the second as if it had been there previously.

ZOOM. A camera movement coming in close to or moving back away from the object—very fast and smooth.

Index

182

SECOND EDITION

UNDERSTANDING TODAY'S THEATRE

By EDWARD A. WRIGHT

Understanding Today's Theatre is for anyone who has ever asked "Why did I like the last play I saw?"... "Why didn't I?"

In the second edition of this volume—revised to cover the most recent developments in the theatre scene—Edward A. Wright, Professor of Theatre Arts, California State College, Long Beach, views the theatre not only as a synthesis of the arts but as an art itself. In an analysis of the elements of all productions—from the classical to the theatre of the absurd—the author provides an inside look at the roles of the playwright, the director, the actors, and the technicians in creating an entertaining work of art.

Understanding Today's Theatre offers the knowledge and the principles that will help the reader toward greater enjoyment and more effective criticism of theatre, from the conventional to the avant-garde.

wood Cliffs, New Jersey

0-13-936237